Attract Money Using the Law of Attraction

'How to" practical step by step daily guide to change your financial life for good

Slavica Bogdanov

This book is dedicated to you
You who have had the courage to change your life!

Congratulations !!

You did the most difficult step:

The first step!

You decided that it is time to change, once and for all

You will get out of your debts for good and accept the
abundance in your life

I am with you now, to help you on your way

AUTHOR NAME

CONTENTS

INTRODUCTION

Thank you for purchasing this book. During my many years of research on success and the law of attraction, I found out what happens when we are looking for something that we wish to obtain. When it comes to money, some universal laws apply specifically.

I wanted to enable the greatest number of people to access wealth and abundance that are part of my daily life. Prosperity is accessible to everyone and I want you too, to have it!

I lived through some serious financial struggles. I know what it is like to collapse under debts and thinking I could never get out. I know what it's like to try to attract wealth while feeling poor. I know what difficulties you live, because I've been there.

I also know that it is possible at any time to change

the circumstances of your life. Sometimes things happen much quicker than we could have even imagined.

What I offer you in this book is not an investment guide on methods to get rich in maybe twenty years. What I offer you is a proven method to use the law of attraction to attract to you all kinds of riches.

No matter where you come from and who you are. Regardless of your past and your education. This book works for everyone. I combined the basic principles of the laws of success and attraction. I added groundbreaking discoveries that have the potential to propel you to the top.

I created a practical guide so that you can incorporate every instruction in your daily routine. Some of the lessons are based on daily habits of the rich and successful so you know how to live wealthy. Other lessons I developed during my many years of research and experimentation on the laws of attraction and success.

Some people-have no difficulty living in wealth and abundance. They are not smarter than you. They simply apply the laws of prosperity in their Lives.

I lived through financial struggles so I know exactly how you feel. I am living proof that my method works. I also dramatically changed the lives of thousands like you during my group and individual coaching.

> "Participating in Slavica Bogdanov's coaching has completely transformed my life. It has opened doors that I never knew existed. It's been a year now and I still see the impact it has had. I live differently and think differently. She made me see how the law of attraction affected my life. I recommend it to everyone. I still do not know how we did it, but since I took her coaching, I made last year's salary in 20 days. I almost hard to believe. " ~ Philippe Lefevre

With extensive research on the law of attraction, and the accumulation of all relevant information about keys to success, I have come to create and use my method to attract wealth and abundance every day. I know you can too.

With my method, you will learn how to free yourself from your fears and thoughts of lack. You will develop enough self-confidence and self-esteem to be able to attract money easily.

As a professional coach, I wanted to add my most successful coaching methods to offer you the best system to use the Law of Attraction for prosperity.

As a coach, I want to push you to excel, to achieve your goal and know that I am with you every step of the way, in spirit and intention. You will have to make significant behavioral changes that will help you earn more, better manage your finances and accumulate extra money.

I created this program to powerfully increase your self love and offer you concrete ways to attract money and keep it.

No matter who you are, by opening this book, I am proud of you. I know how hard it is to make that first step. You've done the hardest part. You have chosen to improve your financial life. You must feel proud of yourself because you decided to change. You have already begun.

Decide that this time, it is for GOOD! Do not put back this book. Bring it with you, wherever you are. It will be your best friend during your positive transformation.

I will be with you during this time as I wish someone could have accompanied me during my self-improvement process.

Every week I'll give you some very easy exercises to do that will aim to change the way you think and act, and open yourself to the laws of success and attraction to bring more money into your life. You will experience major internal changes. The exercises are not complicated but require your participation and full cooperation.

Even if you do not change that behavior, you will have already taken an important step in the right direction and this book will have been worth reading and writing. If you make more, bravo !! The more you do, the changes will be more impressive.

I do not want you to change all your habits and then back to the load to what you have done in the past. I want to see you improve yourself in the long term and for good. Your financial life will be completely transformed. Sure!

Are you ready to change your life? Are you ready to transform you? Would you shine as you shine? You deserve it!

SAY YES !!! AND believe in yourself!

Go say YES !!! YES !!!
Again and again !!

YES !!

This book works even better when you download the full course called "Know it all to Have it all" here www.attractitude.us

1. THE METHOD EXPLAINED

Before jumping into the heart of your money attraction plan, I wanted to explain the methodology that you will follow throughout the process.

As you probably know, the law of attraction is based on the principle that you attract to yourself what you think about most often by deploying more energy.

This book was designed as an intensive coaching program established on 90 days. 90 days seem very long, I know. However, I wanted to let you have sustainable results and positive internal changes that will stay with you throughout your life. The 90 days have already passed many times without your life changing because you haven't done anything. 90 days will pass again without your life changing if you do not adopt this method. One possibility is that your life improves exponentially in the next 90 days. Your life will begin to improve quickly before the end of this book if you decide to follow all prescribed exercises.

This book is created as a daily action plan and a personal diary. The plan allows you to easily track what you need to do each day while the diary allows you to write your successes which will increase with time.

It is essential to do both. The journal allows you to focus on the positive which will attract more of the same

.

The exercises prescribed in the action plan have been created specifically to increase your self love (and feelings that you deserve to be rich) and attract wealth and prosperity.

To do this, we will:
Increase your self-esteem
Define how you want to succeed
Establish a visualization program
Remove your negative thoughts, your mental blocks and learn to respond to these little internal voice that prevent you from moving forward.

You will stop thinking about problems and debts, but change your perspective to focus on solutions and wealth.

Learn how to let go and not be so attached to the outcome.

Develop a method to attract money into your life much easier.

You will have to do specific exercises as you go.

The more you follow the method, the higher your chances of success. By practicing, you get to change your behavior and your thinking.

I want you to be proud of yourself, you have faith in the universe and your open to the love that exists around you!

If this is what you want, say so loud and clear!

Say YES I WANT

I WANT TO LIVE IN ABUNDANCE AND WEALTH !!!.

Yell it if you want. Decide it. Want it!

2 PREPARE FOR CHANGE

The first step to receive anything from the Universe and access to success is knowing what you want exactly.

First of all I want you to promise that you are ready to accumulate more money in your life and that you are ready to do everything in your power to attract that money.

We always start by making a clear and firm decision to change. Even if you have done so in the past, you never have like this.

You need to decide that you want to earn more money (especially not declare that all you want is to pay your debts! But instead that you want to be RICH)

DECIDE! TELL UP AND STRONG: I DECIDE TO CHANGE!

Set your goal:

I want you to write the date before which you would like to receive your desired amount of money. It can be a monthly income or a lump sum. Be realistic. On a scale of 1 to 10, 10 representing an unattainable goal, yours should be around 6-7. You have to believe it is possible.

Confidence in the universe is paramount.

Come On !! I know you'll get there!

Write it here:

I, the undersigned (your name) _____ solemnly declare that I pledge to do everything in my power to attract the amount of _ _ _ _ _ _ _ _ _ _ _ _ by: _____ (date).

Your signature here:
_____

Really awesome !!!

Do you know that 98% of people do not write their goals!
And you just do it !!!
FANTASTIC!

What? You have not written yet? You hesitate?

You have nothing to lose but your debts!
Come On! Write your goal!

GO GO GO !!! SUPER !!! The hard part is done!

You can be stressed for putting on paper a goal that seems so distant, unattainable or impossible. Do not worry. Remember that in the vastness of the universe, ALL is really POSSIBLE!

ALL IS WELL!!!

Soon you'll believe and trust in you and in the Universe (the two go together) so much that circumstances around you will seem to change by themselves.

ALL IS WELL !!!

KNOW WHAT YOU ARE LOOKING FOR EXISTS IN ABUNDANCE !!!

The reason is stronger than the how:

I want you to do the following exercise:

I would like you to name all (at least 25) of the reasons why you want to achieve your goal.

The reasons should not be directed towards others or negative. It should not be to please others or to look like the rich people you hear about, that your parents stop nagging you about your finances or that you pay off your debt ....

List all the reasons.

This list will be your motivator. As soon as you feel like you are going to fail or abandon the journey, come back here and read this list. Remember why you want to succeed.

More your reasons are strong and powerful, the more

your brain will find ways to make you achieve your goals. If your reasons are not sufficiently motivating, there is a good chance that you give up along the way.

You need to change your emotional state of lack to abundance to attract abundance. In writing the reasons why you want to live in abundance, you already start this crucial emotional change.

Well, you do not know what to write. Let me help you a bit.

Here are some reasons that I can think of:

To sleep soundly
To live in relief
To buy anything you want
To be even more generous
To travel
To please your children or your friends

Remember never to write negative reasons such as:
To have no debts
Not to be stressed
In order not to run out of money
Not to end my days in the regrets of a life without money.

Indeed, for the law of attraction, two negative does not make a positive. They are attracting twice as much negativity.

Come on, it's your turn now. Write as many reasons as you can. You can come back here if you find others:

_____

_____
_____
_____
_____
_____
_____
_____
_____
_____
_____
_____
_____
_____
_____
_____
_____
_____
_____
_____
_____
_____
_____
_____
_____
_____
_____
_____
_____
_____
_____

The balance of your reality

This will probably be the first and last time I ask you to look at your reality. The only reason I want you to make your balance sheet is for you to contemplate your success at the end of the program.

Know that most people make the mistake of relying on their " reality " has to judge their potential to improve their financial situation. It is not so! The more you contemplate your situation, the more you will attract the same thing in the future, because of the law of attraction. We'll have to change the perspective to change your financial status.

Some will say that it is difficult not to look at reality as it is. Indeed. It is not easy. However, the more you think about your daily problems, the more you will see what is wrong, you will focus more on your so-called reality, the more it will continue. The solutions are found when looking for solutions and not looking at the problems. With this book you will learn how to change your perspective and align yourself with abundance.

Before starting this extraordinary journey to prosperity, I want you to enter the details of your finances below.

Bank account:
Savings Account:
Accumulated debts:
Property value if there occurs (this is calculated by calculating your mortgage - the resale value of your home):

Your worth:

Don't be afraid to do the math and get clear about your financial state. Know that all successful people know at all times how much they are worth. Do not fear the result. Everything can change quickly.

Once you have made a state of your accounts, you will have less fear of this reality, you will be less tempted to flee it.

The more you feel fear, the more you will attract more

reasons to be afraid. So decide to change your mindset. Many people have been there and you will not die! Trump lost billions! Ford went bankrupt 4 times!

Really, these are just numbers! There's really nothing to be afraid of!

Congratulations !!! Now that it's done, we can change it all!

It's your responsibility

Often when one lives difficult circumstances, it seems easier to blame others.

I often hear people experiencing financial problems blame the state, the economic crisis, lack of proper education in the educational system, lack of resources, lack of rich friends, a past in a poor family ... It seems obvious that the reason of lack of abundance comes from a lot of circumstances you have no control over. THAT IS NOT TRUE !!

In fact, the circumstances are similar to many individuals who live in abundance and prosperity. The economic crisis has not stopped enriching some. Many rich people from poor parents and were raised in disadvantaged areas.

Everything depends on you and the way you react to circumstances. The more you point the finger outside to prove your inability to accumulate money, the more this situation will continue. By blaming others, you give away your power over your future circumstances.

Once you accept your responsibility in what happens to you, you get to take total control over your life. If everything depends on you, it is much easier to predict the future than if everything depends on circumstances which you have no control.

Therefore, now, you must take full responsibility for your financial life. You do not need the enormous burden of guilt. We will later learn how to manage this feeling.

For now, I just want you to accept that you are responsible for your life.

I want you to sign the following oath:

I, the undersigned _____ (your name) takes full responsibility for my financial situation. Thus, I become aware that I have complete control over my finances and that they depend on nobody but me. I have all the power to rebuild my financial life and prosper.

_____ (Your signature)

Do you really like the money?

I would like you to take a moment to ask yourself how you felt when reading words such as " rich " or ',wealthy". Deep inside you, did you feel hatred for rich people, envy, jealousy or anger? Have you had thoughts such as: " For sure they have money, they took advantage of others ", " the rich get richer, the poor get poorer ", " the rich have good accounting and not me ", " they are lucky ", " they work all the time ", " they are greedy and do not enjoy life. "

How do you feel when you think about wealth? Could you take a few minutes to write down all the negative thoughts that come up when you think the rich or wealthy.

Those are some of your blocs to riches:

_____

_____
_____
_____
_____
_____
_____
_____
_____
_____
_____
_____
_____
_____
_____
_____
_____
_____
_____

Know that rich people, except for the way they respect their money, do not differ from you. Some are nice people, friendly, generous, wicked, mean or perverse, ... in all levels of wealth. I've realized that money only increases the qualities or defects that you already have within you. Ordinary people, generous and good remain so, with or without money. Individuals who are already wicked, bitter, greedy, will be at all times of their lives, no matter what their financial circumstances are..

If you think rich people are worse than others, you may unconsciously fear that some of your faults will increase with prosperity.

I advise you to look out your flaws and learn to appreciate them. Find the qualities of your faults. Find how these defects serve you. If they do not serve you, then change them!! Everyone can change at any time.

I noticed that 2 faults often resulted in financial problems: arrogance (lack of humility) and lack of gratitude.

Take the time to write down your flaws. You will have less fear of becoming a 'villain' rich if you notice, basically, you're really a good person.

_____

_____

_____

_____

_____

_____

_____

_____

How do you handle money? If you scrunch your bills, throw them in a pot without counting them, wasting them ... It goes without saying that you treat money without respect and you offer it no love.

As absurd as it may seem, the money is an energy that responds extremely well to love. The more you love your money (not idolize it of course), the more you will accumulate it. The more you love the sources of your income, the more you accumulate wealth.

From now on, I would like you to pay attention to your money. I would like you pile it nicely, place it carefully in your wallet, as you pay attention to a loved one that you would like to attract into your life. These small gestures will have great consequences. Money is energy, nothing more or less. Treat that energy kindly and you will not repel it.

A first step towards abundance

You can never find prosperity when thinking about poverty and lack. Therefore, you must stop rehashing all financial ills plaguing your existence.

The best way to know if you think of wealth or abundance is to listen to your feelings. When your stomach is tied, it is obvious that you think about money missing in our life.

You must change this !! The only way to attract the best is to think the best and feel your best. So how do you react when you are stressed and think only about debts ?? It is good practice to change your thoughts from 'I do not want' 'to' 'I want.' '

The first you have to promise that you will practice to replace all your thoughts from lack to prosperity thoughts.

When you feel oppressed, stop and examine your thinking. If you think of debt, decide to change and think of the money that comes to you.

You may think that doing this is ridiculous and to imagine that simply changing your mind state can transform your financial statement is silly. Well, IT'S POWERFUL !! Through the law of attraction, what you think about most is what you will attract the most.

The more you put your attention on what you do not want, the more you attract it! It is as if you are deploying a large banner: " problems are welcomed here. " You will find that people who speak more about wealth are those who live more abundantly.

Take a small paper, cardboard or wear a rubber band around the wrist that will remind you to stay focused on wealthy thoughts. When you feel stressed, stop and say out loud what you want and not what you do not want. If necessary, review the reasons why you want more money. Thus, you will change your emotional, spiritual and intellectual states which will effectively change your field of attraction.

You may not know it, but you are connected to an endless source of information and intelligence. Some call it the soul, others God. For others, it is the power of this amazing machine that we call the brain. One thing is certain, no matter how you name it, this part of you contains all solutions for you to attain prosperity.

An extremely powerful way to activate this power in you is simply by asking and letting it come up with solutions without your conscious self involved. As soon as you start to think in fear by looking only at the problem, you block the force of this important part of your being. You confuse your vision as you fill it with doubts and fears.

A good way to let it go and let it work so the law of attraction and your inner strength is to repeat frequently:

" I leave the burden of financial problems to the God in me and I walk forward now free of this difficulty before me! "

Write this sentence on a card and carry it with you. When you feel that you are unable to think of possible solutions, say that sentence out loud with a strong intention.

The problems of addiction

Before proceeding further, I would like to address a serious issue that is central to your money attraction.

If you drink alone, in excess, if you can not go a week without a drink, I strongly advise you to address this issue first. This applies also if you have gambling problems (which can not be controlled). If you smoke, I would strongly advise you to stop.

If you have one or more symptoms that you would show you have an addiction, you must get rid of it. Not only they are contrary to prosperity, but the addiction is related to a much deeper problem that will prevent you to thrive.

Sometimes unconscious deep sense of guilt will develop. Guilt is one of the biggest causes of low self-esteem. Self-esteem is crucial to your success. Indeed, without self love, you will not think you deserve your due and therefore will not attract it.

Addiction is often a symptom of a lack of deep love. I've solved some addiction problems by substantially increasing self-esteem of my coaching clients. If you follow all the prescribed exercises in this book (especially the first) you will improve your self-esteem. However, you must completely get rid of addiction in order to thrive. You may say that some people are rich and alcoholics. It is true, but the prosperity and abundance also include health. These people lack another important part of the whole called "success".

Money is an energy that helps provide you much good, but it is not the most important thing in life. If you do not have your health, millions of dollars will lose their luster and you will exchange them willingly for a miracle cure.

You must develop your love of you and love begins by avoiding excess. I beg you to get rid of them at the earliest.

The advantages of your disadvantages

The exercise that follows will allow you to remove the first blocks that prevent you from moving forward.

You need to understand this. If you do not have the salary, income or financial statement that you want, it's because, deep inside you, you find benefits to living in this situation that you might not ready to give up.

You do not perhaps realize, but it is clear that you are where you are because you want to. It is not always easy to accept, but it is really so. Nobody stays where they are if there are no benefits at all. These may be unconscious, but they exist nonetheless. You would not be where you are if you did not like it at all. It is important that you accept the following concept in order to continue.

All circumstances have advantages of disadvantages. It is sometimes hard to accept that we love to complain and it is for this reason that one remains in an unpleasant situation. It is sometimes difficult to accept that part of yourself loves the problem because, without it, you should face the unknown: the comfort, happiness, a life without worry.

The following exercise is used to detect these reasons (benefits) and turn them into benefits incurred when you are rich.

I would like you to name all the benefits that you find to be poor, in debt or in a negative financial situation.

This exercise will unlock the first concepts that prevent you from living in prosperity. This is a very important exercise so I strongly urge you not to skip it. Take your time and come back regularly to ensure that you do not skid again.

I offer you a few examples to help you.

I do not have to manage a lot of money
I will not receive more bills related to my increase in spending
I can complain incessantly
I have the support of my friends in the same situation as myself
I keep my importance
My relatives did not feel threatened by my success
That's all I know and that is reassuring
I do not know what I will do with a lot of money
I do not have to face the fear of being alone
I would not be disappointed by the success that can lead me to failure again
I do not have to face my fear of failure

Your turn:

_____

_____

_____

_____

_____

_____

_____

_____

_____

_____

_____

_____

_____

_____

_____

_____

_____

_____

_____

_____

_____

_____

Now I would like you replace these advantages by advantages of being rich. For example:

That's all I know: I want to develop my knowledge of the life of the rich

I do not know what I will do with much money: I'll learn to spend it wisely and save a lot

I do not have to face the fear of being alone: I will have new rich friends

I will not be disappointed by the success that can bring me to failure again: I can keep my wealth forever.

Your turn:

_____

_____

_____

_____

_____

_____

_____

_____

_____

_____

_____

_____

_____

_____
_____
_____
_____
_____
_____
_____
_____
_____

Now you will find new benefits, those linked to your wealth. For example:

I will live in relief
I do not have to deprive myself
My children will benefit from it
I will be loved for who I am, a successful individual

Some reasons may resemble what you've written in the section of " why " that motivate you. Repeat as necessary.

_____
_____
_____
_____
_____
_____
_____
_____
_____
_____
_____
_____
_____
_____
_____
_____

The next exercise is also intended to get rid of a huge mental block. Few people talk about it, but it is vital.

Many people live their lives vicariously. They depend on "what will people say" and "what is expected of me.' ' One of the biggest bottlenecks in using the law of attraction in a positive way is that many people fail to succeed in order not to harm a loved one. People often sabotage their success because subconsciously they do not wish to overshadow a close family member or an old friend.

Have you noticed how anger can rise in you when you act, in spite of you, to please others, especially if you are doing something you dislike, or you take the time that you wanted to give yourself for another more significant activity. You feel compelled, or because the other did a favor for you in the past and ask you subtly to return the favor, or because it is a close relative to whom you do not have the strength to say " No '.

Likewise, you may feel a lot of frustration when you help someone " who did not deserve it. " These tantrums are frequently caused by the distortion between your needs and giving "too much" to others. The more you will feel " taxed " the more you will be frustrated.

The need to please a loved one can cause real blocking (often unconscious) to manifest your desire. For one, you do not want to disappoint or displease the beloved.

Sometimes a close relative will give you an advice about what to do and you feel compelled to follow it. It is possible that you feel confronted with parental authority remembering the orders you had to obey as a child.

This situation could lead you to an internal conflict. You want to be successful and achieve your goals, but you also want to be loved and accepted by people who are important to you.

This can result in the inability to earn more money because, for example, a parent or close friend would feel " useless ", because its role was limited to cheer you up or help you financially.

Here is an example of a client that was helping his mother unconsciously. The relationship between mother and son was undermined. The mother felt important in the life of her son when she could help him by lending him money. Although the pride of the man was injured (which also demolished self-esteem) and that he hated the help his mother was giving, he would not (unconsciously) disparaging to his mother her role of protector .

Maternal love was expressed by the money offered and the man did not want to, without even realizing it, wound the mother by being able to be in charge of his finances. So he continued to create situations where financial assistance from the mother was required. Thus, the mother found her loving role, helping and caring. We managed to change this when the client became aware of this relationship and offered another role of importance to his mother. He regularly asks her opinion, required her assistance in various tasks. The mother maintained her role without influencing the financial life of her son.

For the next exercise, ask yourself, about your financial

situation: Who enjoys it the most? Ask yourself also this question: 'If I can achieve this prosperity, who could feel hurt and why? Who already warned me not to try to be richer and explained why I can't? Who would feel belittled or injured, and why? "

When you find the name of the person who causes conflict in you, write him or her a letter. This is often of someone very close to you that you love and respect. You will not need to give that person the letter. The only action of writing it can cause a deep liberating change in you. You will probably have to write to more than one person.

In this letter you must:
- Name the person concerned
- Write the goal you want to achieve
- Put on paper the inconvenience this may cause to the person to whom you are writing the letter. You can start by " Although my success will cause you ... " listing the effects that could be perceived as negative. Add a maximum of details. Describe any past examples that lead you to believe that you are right.
- Write all the other benefits that could comet following your success.
- Forgive the other person's limitations and fears
- Giving back to the other the responsibility of his or her life. You do not have to act on regrets or desires of others or build your life according to the image they liked most or would be socially accepted.
- Thank the other of its continuous and unconditional love. Free yourself and move forward with your plans.

Start here:

_____

_____

_____

_____

_____

_____

_____

_____

_____

_____

_____

_____

_____

_____

_____

_____

_____

_____

_____

_____

_____

_____

_____

_____

_____

_____

_____

_____

_____

_____

_____

_____

_____

_____

_____

_____

Once completed, you can destroy the letter. And release the block that prevented you from moving forward. This exercise effectively solves a blockage preventing the operation of the positive law of attraction. Unfortunately, sometimes the ties are very deep and some people can be induced to imagine the advice and criticism from relatives by deduction without even having shared their projects. If you feel that you have high self-sabotage, try doing the letter often. You'll feel liberated. Do the exercise for each person as many times as needed until you feel free to live according to your own choice.

The perfect day

Once you have written what motivates you to change, we will move to this next exercise.

I would like you to describe your perfect day. I would like you to describe what will it look like once you have reached your goal.

How will you feel?
How do you walk?
What will you do that you do now?
Where will you go?
Where will you be?
What will you do differently?

I want you to feel good and happy. I want you to describe your dream life. The dream that causes a wide smile on your beautiful face.

This exercise is quite easy and only requires a little imagination. If you do not feel inspired, fear not, the ideas will come to you.

If you really feel that no idea comes to mind, I suggest

you look at some of your favorite films to inspire you a little.

You can copy plots here and there to create your own ideal history.

Take your time. Come back here often. This will be your film project of the happy times to come!

_____

_____

_____

_____

_____

_____

_____

_____

_____

_____

_____

_____

_____

_____

_____

_____

_____

_____

_____

_____

_____

_____

_____

_____

_____

_____

_____

_____

_____

_____

_____

_____

_____

_____

_____

_____

_____

_____

_____

_____

_____

_____

_____

_____

_____

_____

_____

_____

_____

_____

_____

_____

Get rid of other mental blocks:

In this session, I would like you to speak about all the reasons why you have not achieved your financial goal yet.

This is not about he advantages of staying where you are (as in the previous exercise), but really deep reasons why you are not rich yet.

Be honest. I will not tell anyone.

Is it because you think you do not deserve it?
You think you cannot?
You failed and you are afraid to fail again?
You experienced traumas in your family and are afraid to relive those again?
You do not have enough education ...?

I would like you to explain all the reasons why you are still in this financial situation today.

By illuminating the reasons that block you, you will be better able to address them and face them. Thus, you will have less mental blocks that prevent you from moving forward. You will have less fear.

The darkness can not exist in the light!

Come On !! Take the time to do this!

_____

_____
_____
_____
_____
_____
_____
_____
_____
_____
_____
_____

_____
_____
_____
_____
_____
_____
_____
_____
_____
_____
_____
_____
_____
_____
_____
_____
_____
_____
_____
_____
_____
_____
_____
_____
_____
_____
_____
_____
_____

THIS IS AWESOME !!!

I love you for doing it all !! Applaud yourself! Say YES !!

Say YES
Say YES
Say YES !!!!!

I can do it
I can do it
I WILL DO IT !!!

Say it with me! Stand straight up and say it loud. Say it and repeat it: YES you will get there!

You will get there!
Slowly but surely!

You are OK and I love you!

Now that you know what is blocking you, I want you to explain in a few sentences why now you WILL change your life!

For example, if you said earlier that you failed in the past due to bad investments or spending too much, say that this time you will get there.

Write down the reasons, as this will play a lot in the

way you act in the future. By writing your changes to how you behave about past negative reasons, you make a first giant step towards a future positive transformation.

Moreover, confront your fears:

Not to be in control (at least when things go wrong you know things are bad)

Having time to think about success

Being rich with poor friends (you can advise them and help them)

Having confidence in the future

Being yourself

It is normal to be afraid. The real success is to know your fears and move forward in spite of them.

The best way to proceed is to remember the reasons why you want a prosperous life. If your reasons are stronger than your fears, you will advance more quickly.

_____

_____

_____

_____

_____

_____

_____

_____

_____

_____

_____

_____

_____

_____

_____

_____

_____
_____
_____
_____
_____
_____
_____
_____
_____
_____
_____
_____
_____
_____
_____
_____
_____
_____
_____
_____
_____
_____
_____

Visualize

On the next two pages, I want you to stick pictures of what abundance means for you. You can cut illustrations from magazines: the house in which you will live, the clothes you want to wear or activities that you can do now with more money. You can even paste an image of the trips you want to take, dining out ...

You can even decide to draw the images (which has even more impact) of what a prosperous life means to you.

Check back regularly for these inspiring images to motivate you to continue.

You will visualize every day for 10 to 15 minutes. Closing her eyes, you imagine you live moments of happiness with your fortune. This should not be perceived as a chore, but rather as happiness. The more the associated feelings will stronger, the more the law of attraction will work.

You are in control and responsible for your life. You can do it!

So with that in mind, we continue.

Say YES!

I can do it!
I will do it!
And you will do it !!!

Slavica Bogdanov

The 100 dollars bill

The more you feel richer, the more wealth you attract. If you feel poor, you attract more reasons to feel poor. The following simple exercise will help you feel much richer.

I want you to insert the biggest bill you can in your wallet. If you can only afford 20 dollars, then put only 20 dollars. With time, you will be able to have much more in your pocket.

It is important not to spend it. All you'll do is place it prominently to always be able to see it when you shop. Do not spend it, in any case.

If you are able to have 100 dollars, you will mentally do the following exercise (adjust it depending on the amount that you have available).

You will frequently walk in department stores and make imaginary purchases in the amount of the bill you have at your disposal. You choose what you want and, once that is done, I want you to say 'I can offer myself (I can afford it) all this, but I choose not to buy it.' ' Repeat this exercise frequently.

It will produce two important things: the first is that it will change your internal monologue, namely 'oh no, it's too expensive, I cannot buy it" which by the Law of Attraction draws you over similar circumstances.

The second beneficial effect is also important. The brain works like a calculator. The more you repeat a sentence, the more it gains value neurologically. For example, if you have a chore to do and you think about it all the time, it will become monumental. That's why so many people fall into procrastination.

If you keep saying you have 100 dollars to spend, the brain will accumulate this amount and add it to the previous one. It's something that bears fruit, because the more your brain will accumulate the sum, the more you will feel rich. Therefore, through the law of attraction, you attract more money.

I am aware that some of these exercises seem so simple that you might think they are not worth the trouble of being executed. I know, because I was thinking the same thing. The value of my bank account has improved greatly when I started to practice. If you do not like your current financial situation, I advise you to try what I say. You have nothing to lose and a lot of money to win.

Last steps before the plunge:

Dealing with fear:

Everyone is afraid. The rich also have to deal with this feeling. One big difference is that successful people understand the role of fear. This is telling you that you going over the limits (imagined or real) that you are not used to go over. Getting out of your comfort zone is scary. However, it is only out of your comfort zone that you will manage to surpass yourself and overcome your problems.

If, for a moment only, you observe your life as would someone from the outside, without feeling personally concerned, you will see that all your problems are only experiments aimed to make you evolve. Sometimes you attract to yourself the most difficult circumstances, because you think you deserve them or feel the need to be punished. In general, the problems will be solved forever and you will grow every time a little more.

The next time you encounter a problem, ask yourself what positive aspects it may contain. Every problem can be overcome when you grow. Every problem you are experiencing has already been experienced by someone else and resolved. Therefore, instead of bending to fear and feeling terrified by your financial problems, detach yourself from those feelings and put yourself in search of solutions. Go meet specialists, read on a topic that interests you to solve your problem. It is so easy these days to find the answers quickly. No longer live as a victim, but assume the role of actor of your life and decide to change it.

Successful people look at problems as simple equations to solve. They learn what they need to learn, to grow and thus overcome the problem.

Write below what you most fear. What are the biggest problems you have to overcome and write off 'a solution exists, "I'll find it.' ' You can write: " I decided that the solution presents itself to me, I release myself from this problem. "

_____

_____
_____
_____
_____
_____
_____
_____
_____
_____
_____
_____
_____
_____
_____
_____
_____
_____
_____
_____
_____
_____
_____
_____

_____
_____
_____
_____
_____
_____
_____
_____
_____
_____
_____
_____
_____
_____
_____
_____
_____

Pretend:

An effective method to accelerate the process of the law of attraction is to act as if you had already achieved your outcome.

I would like you to pay attention to the way you live every day and prepare your way of life to include fortune. Act, talk, walk, experience the success and prosperity.

The rich think before they spend, do not like to waste, invest more money in better quality goods, calculate their budget, calculate their costs, first think of saving money, spending less they save more, pay attention to their properties so they last longer, repair instead of buying new, dress in finer clothes, constantly educate themselves on new ways of investing, constantly calculate the value of what they have or what they want to own, think long term rather than immediate gratification, plan their spending and use credit wisely to avoid paying interest.

Starting today, you will ALWAYS be careful what you are doing. You must be ready to become rich. You are already rich, you have to exert yourself.

Play rich and you will get rich!

Starting today, you began a countdown of your miserable state. You are on the path to prosperity. Look at your current life and know that it will soon be different. You want to prepare yourself mentally to the new life that awaits you.

9 YOUR PROGRAM TO WEALTH

This program consists of a mix of exercises that cause the law of attraction to increase your wealth and a daily diary that will allow you to increase your cash inflows.

Starting today, you'll pay attention to all the signs of abundance around you and note them in your journal. This week (and for the rest of the program), I want you to write everything that relates to money. Everything !!

This is serious !!!

Carry this book with you. At worst, have a notepad and pen at all times all the signs that you see that shows you that you receive money or that abundance exists.

Usually, my clients tell me they see nothing, no sign. You have just not accustomed your eyes to detect abundance. The more you get used to look at the wealth and not its lack, the more you will attract it.

Examples of signs of abundance:
The money you receive or you find
Positive conversations with respect to finances
Rich people you meet
ALL that includes any sign of abundance.

I want you to also pay attention to how you feel when you watch the rich people. Are you sad, envious or angry?

I would like you to bless ALL rich people you meet.

When you envy someone rich, you send a sign of lack to the Universe. You denigrate abundance. Envying others, you tell the Universe that you lack the money. Therefore, the Universe will send you more of this lack.

You will do this first exercise during the first 7 days. Eventually, I want you to continue to write anything that relates to money, every day, all the time. In this book.

In addition, each day you will write all the money you spend. The money spent and invoices received are all signs of abundance. Often people are angry to receive bills and thus block the flow of the Universe. In fact, you should develop gratitude for bills received. Without them, you would not have electricity, telephone, hot water ... so thank the abundance that surrounds you by thanking the bills you receive. On each of them, write in clearly visible letters: " Thanks for the money. "

You will also put you to record your expenses. Rich people look straight, without fear, at all aspects of their finances. Expenditures are a part of that. Moreover, by recording your expenses, you will begin to reduce them unconsciously, because you will find where you exaggerate and spend too much.

A golden rule to get rich

There is a golden rule to accumulate wealth: ALWAYS pay yourself first. This means that you must, from now on (if not already) open a savings account. 10% of EVERYTHING you earn (net) must be put into that account as soon as you receive it.

Most people wait to the end of the month to see if they still have a few pennies to spare. Rich people pay, themselves, and save at the source immediately. This is the principle of the hen with the golden eggs.

You must create a fund that will one day work for you. By removing 10% of your income from the source, you'll not think of lack and you will quickly earn money.

This money will work one day for you and thus you will not have to work for your money. The goose that lays golden eggs will offer you monthly income. It is therefore important to NEVER spend the money saved, but enjoy only its interests. Initially, the concept of living for your interests seems distant. Know that time passes anyway and it is better that you start saving right away.

Moreover, the fact of saving changes your perception and attention. Instead of constantly be thinking about your debts and bills to pay, you are going to start thinking and watching the money accumulated. Your energy will change and become more positive. Through the law of attraction, you will begin to accumulate more money. If you think you save, you attract reasons to save. If you think to spend (even if it is thinking that you do not want more debt or you do not want more problems), you will attract more reasons to spend.

The law of attraction works by attracting to you what you think about most. If you avoid dealing with a problem, and if you reject it, you fight against a problem, you will attract more of the same. The law of attraction does not know negation and, therefore, sends you what you think about the most even if you do not want it.

It is important to ALWAYS be thinking about what you want. If a debt you thought crosses your mind, replicate immediately by offering a thought of prosperity and abundance. Repeat your goal (the one you entered at the beginning of this book) as many times as you can.

If 10% of your income seems too big to save initially, then save 5%. No matter the amount, SAVE !!!

You will greatly change the focus of your energy and you will go to accumulate more and more money and to think in terms of increasingly positive thoughts and outcomes.

Financial management makes rich

If you are not able to manage the finances you have today, how do you what the Universe to send you more money. The Universe loves simplicity. If you find your life complicated with the finances you have, you do not draw more simplicity by adding more money. If you feel like you have money problems, you will subconsciously feel like more money means more problems..

The new money does not necessarily mean simplifying your finances. On the contrary. The more you have a large income, you will need to manage more intelligently: namely reinvesting, develop an accounting system, pay higher taxes, manage your investments (which require time) ...

You can now prove to the Universe (and to your subconscious mind) that you're a good money manager through the following exercise:

Get yourself 6 jars. In the future, these jars will be

replaced by bank accounts. You will fill these jars as follows, once a week. The importance lies in regularity to the exercise and precise division of the amount. The size of the amount does not matter. The Universe does not see much difference between 10 dollars and one million. It is only a succession of added 0. In fact, for the Universe, bringing you more does not require much energy. Look at the infinity of the universe. Your wishes are similar to those of an ant. The only block lies in your ability to accept that abundance.

You can start by allocating an amount of 10 dollars, then slowly divide all your net income at source. It is very important to do this exercise every week, regardless of how frequently you receive your income.

Distribution of money:
10% savings (goose that lays golden eggs)
55% necessities (rent, mortgage, current necessary expenditure ...)
5% to charity
10% Education (it is important to always reinvest in yourself, in your personal development)
10% medium-term investment (greater expenditure planned or repayment of credit cards)
10% games and pleasures (anything that is not part of necessities: dining out, fun, massages, buying clothes for fun and not work, beauty care, not health ...)

CAUTION:

The 10% allocated to the games and pleasures MUST be followed !! You do not want to deprive yourself because, over time, you will get pleasure out of spite and spend in instant pleasure that will not be fully felt.

Also, do not spend more than 10% for fun. Many

people make a mistake without even knowing it (you will realize by writing your daily expenses): a small coffee with cream here, a small restaurant out here and there, a small sweater here, a massage there ... Soon the 10% becomes 20 or 30%. This has two disastrous effects on your finances:

- You prove that you do not think long-term and thus block the attraction of more money
- You enjoy yourself without having really deserved it, which has the effect of causing you unconscious guilt, which ruins your self esteem ...

In addition, you do not fully enjoy this fun spending because you do it often without really allowing it. The next time you are spending your pleasure amount, I want you jump for joy, as you do with all your heart, like a child who would break the piggy bank to have fun to the fullest. Obviously, the money spent must be done so in cash and not via a plastic card. You will live and much more satisfaction.

The expense should be fun once a month. Build up your jar, and once per month, take all the money accumulated and offer yourself a good time.

I know that many of you who are reading this book cannot, at present separate all your income as indicated, as the majority goes either to the necessities or debts.

But I want you to assiduously separate an amount with which you feel comfortable with, even if it is only 10 dollars. With time, you will be able to separate more and more money. By showing the world that you are able to manage your finances, you will receive more money to manage.

Pay particular attention to your goose that lays golden

eggs to change your emotional state and pay more attention to the accumulation of money rather than its lack. Through the law of attraction, you will begin to attract more systematically money saved.

Overwhelmed by bills to pay: What Works?

It is very difficult to think of abundance when we feel overwhelmed by bills or problems to manage. I know, I've been there.

I command you this fundamental exercise.

Fill out the following :

Bill from	Total amount to pay	Limit for payment	Minimum to pay

Duplicate this table in a notebook to keep it up to date. Here's what you need to do.

You will write all the bills you have to pay. Then all the total amounts to be paid. Then, the due date for payment. Finally, you indicate minimum amounts that are required.

I want you to organize invoices starting with the ones you that have the lowest balance. Make it in the following order:

The total amount is lower than the lowest minimum amount to be paid
Minimum amount to pay the lowest to highest
Due date of invoices

You will start paying the full amount the first (smallest consequently). I would like, if possible, you add a few extra dollars to pay a little more than the minimum.

You'll do this until you are no longer able to pay the amounts indicated. Remember to keep some money for your necessities of the coming months.

Even if it seems that you still have many bills, do not worry, you've reversed the machines very quickly.

If you have credit cards, DO NOT USE THEM ANYMORE UNTIL YOU HAVE FULLY PAID THEM. For credit cards with high interest rates, cancel them as soon as you have paid them. Yes, you will probably tighten your belts a little. Yes, you may not be able to spoil your children as much, but it will teach them financial responsibility that will bring them much more than gifts you buy them on credit.

By doing this simple exercise, you accomplish an immense step towards your financial success. Why? Behold, when you start to repay entirely the same invoice and adding a small amount more, you take control of your finances. You suddenly feel that you are no longer a fearful victim who does not face up to your responsibilities, but more like an individual larger than his problems who is able to overpower his financial troubles.

You send therefore a completely different energy in the universe. You pay your bills. Of course, you do not have all paid on the spot. With time, you will see that their quantity will decrease substantially.

If, for example, you receive a phone bill of 50 dollars and put 51 dollars down, you have the following month a bill with 49 dollars to pay. This seems very minimal, but for the Universe, you send a very different energy.

The second thing to do is to pay your bills as SOON as you receive them. Open the envelope immediately. Thus, you face your fears and reduce the impact they will have. The more you feel fear, the more you attract more reasons to be afraid. By paying your bills early, you will feel in control.

Remember to thank the bill, because it is proof that you live in abundance, you received a valuable service and that you can pay. Write on the invoice: 'thank you for the money'

We start the program:

From now on, I'll give you a few mental exercises easy to do, but essential to your success.

You will do what is stated in this book at the time specified for best results. You can also obtain the complete method by going to: http://attractitude.us

Come On! Let's start! No reason to stop now! You've done the hard part!

You are OK !!
You are quite right as you are!
And I love you!

The first exercise is about love

Self-love is a fundamental pillar of success. Unfortunately, over 80% of the population suffers from not loving themselves enough to receive all the abundance and feel that they are not enough (rich enough, beautiful enough, smart enough, educated enough ...).

But, you're great, you're already perfect and wealth already exists around you. What often blocks people's ability to receive that abundance is often related to the false impression of not deserving it.

Everyone attaches a certain value (monetary or otherwise). The less your self esteem, the less you think you're worth and the less you earn. You may arrive to increase your wealth for a time, until the gap between what you think your worth and what you see widens. From that moment you will proceed to self-sabotage: you will destroy what you have built up in order to return to the level you think you deserve. The only way out of this trap is to change the value you have in your eyes.

In addition, learning to love yourself more, You will depend much less on the love of others and the opinions of others. Therefore, you will no longer feel afraid of being abandoned if you achieve more success. The law of attraction attracts to you what scares you. The more you will trust in yourself, the less you fear. By loving, you release most fears that blocked your openness to money. Therefore the following exercises are very important.

Super. Let's start! During this first week, we will only make an honest statement of your habits.

The first thing you will do is to list all your flaws. Be honest and comprehensive.

For each default, you'll find the quality that is attached and the reason that causes this fault that serves you. If you find any defects that you really hate, I want you to choose one at a time that you will replace by a quality. You always have the option to change. It is up to you.

For example, if you are stubborn, you can say that you are persistent. If you are selfish, you can say that you love yourself first in order to provide more love to others thereafter.

It is necessary to love yourself completely and unconditionally. Go ahead, write down all your flaws by answering them, turning:

_____

_____

_____

_____

_____

_____

_____

_____

_____

_____

_____

_____

_____

_____

_____

Now I want you to choose 10 of your successes and your 5 defeats. The successes will enable you to think positively of yourself and defeats to know that you have overcome other obstacles in the past. Through your losses, you will learn what habits you need to change and what mistakes to avoid.

Come On. Take your time. Each exercise is

fundamental and you will advance to the path of success.

_____
_____
_____
_____
_____
_____
_____
_____
_____
_____
_____
_____
_____
_____
_____
_____
_____
_____
_____
_____
_____
_____

_____

First daily exercise:

Exercise of love. I love myself, I'd like you to allow two long minutes every morning to look yourself in the eyes in the mirror and say: " I LOVE YOU " really feel it and name yourself. Say it as if you would say those words to the person most dear to your heart!

You need to reconnect to your inner child who needs love. This love is a healer and will allow you to rebuild your confidence.

Being 'enough', loved or feeling significant is fundamental and necessary to our vitality and happiness. 90% of people suffer from not feeling quite significant enough. This feeling comes from a deep wound in childhood during which the child has associated a gesture or a word from a parent or guardian to a form of non-merit love. Each punishment that the child does not understand and considers unjustified digs the gap of lack of love.

You will notice that it's very powerful. You may not be able to do it for 2 minutes at first, but do your best to stay as long as you can. You can also add "I forgive you". Measure the time if necessary to be sure to offer you the love you need.

This works a lot and has healing effects for the soul. When you are accustomed to repeating this sentence over and over, I want you to add: " you're great", " you're safe. " With your name. EVERY MORNING from now on. Treat yourself to this special attention. In the audio program called "Know it all to have it all" at http://attractitude.us, I explain in detail why this is so important. The more you do it, the more you will see miracles in your life.

Write it on a sticky paper to remind you what you need to say.

Start your first week.

YOU CAN DO THAT !!
IT'S EASY

Say YES!
Say YES !!!!

Say YES and think it really !!!

Write the date before each day
Day 1: _____

Exercise " I love myself " in front of the mirror in the morning

Visualize for 10-15 minutes

Below is to serve as a diary of all signs of abundance you see:

_____
_____
_____
_____
_____
_____
_____
_____
_____
_____
_____
_____
_____
_____
_____
_____
_____
_____
_____
_____
_____
_____
_____
_____
_____
_____

Write the date before each day

Day 2: _____

Exercise " I love myself " in front of the mirror in the morning

Visualize for 10-15 minutes

Below is to serve as a diary of all signs of abundance you see:

_____

_____

_____

_____

_____

_____

_____

_____

_____

_____

_____

_____

_____

_____

_____

_____

_____

_____

_____

_____

_____

_____

_____

_____

Write the date before each day

Day 3: _____

Exercise " I love myself " in front of the mirror in the morning

Visualize for 10-15 minutes

Below is to serve as a diary of all signs of abundance you see:

_____

_____

_____

_____

_____

_____

_____

_____

_____

_____

_____

_____

_____

_____

_____

_____

_____

_____

_____

_____

_____

_____

_____

_____

Write the date before each day

Day 4: _____

Exercise " I love myself " in front of the mirror in the

morning
    Visualize for 10-15 minutes

Below is to serve as a diary of all signs of abundance you see:

_____

_____

_____

_____

_____

_____

_____

_____

_____

_____

_____

_____

_____

_____

_____

_____

_____

_____

_____

_____

_____

_____

_____

_____

_____

Write the date before each day
    Day 5: _____
    Exercise " I love myself " in front of the mirror in the morning
    Visualize for 10-15 minutes

Below is to serve as a diary of all signs of abundance you see:

_____
_____
_____
_____
_____
_____
_____
_____
_____
_____
_____
_____
_____
_____
_____
_____
_____
_____
_____
_____
_____
_____
_____
_____
_____
_____
_____
_____
_____

Write the date before each day

Day 6: _____

Exercise " I love myself " in front of the mirror in the morning

Visualize for 10-15 minutes

Below is to serve as a diary of all signs of abundance you see:

_____
_____
_____
_____
_____
_____
_____
_____
_____
_____
_____
_____
_____
_____
_____
_____
_____
_____
_____
_____
_____
_____
_____
_____
_____
_____
_____
_____

Write the date before each day
    Day 7: _____
    Exercise " I love myself " in front of the mirror in the morning
    Visualize for 10-15 minutes

Below is to serve as a diary of all signs of abundance

you see:

_____

_____

_____

_____

_____

_____

_____

_____

_____

_____

_____

_____

_____

_____

_____

_____

_____

_____

_____

_____

_____

_____

_____

_____

_____

_____

_CONGRATULATIONS !!
YOU HAVE STARTED YOUR JOURNEY !!

I want you to take the time to describe how you feel.

Do you think you have done your best with your morning exercise? If this is not the case, it does not matter, you will do better and better. Know that you are loved anyway.

Yes. I love you anyway.
You will practice more with the coming weeks.

Have you noticed many signs of abundance around you?

Have you paid attention to the way you feel about rich people?

Take the time to write a summary of your thoughts of the week to see what you can improve.

_____

_____

_____

_____

_____

_____

_____

_____

_____

_____

_____

_____

_____

_____

_____

_____

_____

_____

_____

_____

_____

_____

_____

_____

_____

_____

_____

_____

For the week number 2, you will add two tiny little changes in your habits. They are simple and seem ridiculous. But, it is ESSENTIAL that you add them.

The first change is about order.
Every day, you will ensure that your home is tidy. I want you to take time each day to sort, organize, get rid of things that no longer serve you.

You will create a filing system, a folder for each type of expenditure and bills you incur. You will also create a series of folders for different incoming moneys you expect or hope for. You can include your salary or your sales and also a file for surprising money inflows. Create as many folders as you want where plenty of cash will be available to file.

You need to get rid of the old, which is full of connotation of lack and scarcity to make room for the abundance that will come in your life. The universe loves order. And your brain too. Your ideas will be much clearer if you live in an organized place.

The other reason to have an orderly life that is paramount, it is for a matter of self-esteem. It is important that you become aware that you have to behave towards yourself as you would with best friend.

If you go to a person that you like and it's always a mess at home, you will develop a negative image of this person. Similarly, unconsciously, you will develop a negative image of yourself if you still live in disorder.

If you're the type to do massive spring cleaning when

entertaining guests, be aware that this indicates a low self esteem. Why do you put the other people at a higher level of importance? You should treat yourself better than anyone else and take the time to pamper yourself.

The law of attraction works much better when everything is ordered. The universe loves storage and cleanliness. You will be more in line with strong energy of attraction if you are organized.

I want you to spend an hour a day on housework (your files, photos, videos, clothing ...) You can do it while watching TV. It's easy to find an hour in the day.

OK, I agree, this might not be that easy at first. You are perhaps familiar with your junk or disorder. So obviously it's hard to stop. But remember, you love yourself! You want to give you love and pay attention to your environment by offering what is the best.

The second element you need to learn is about changing the way you breathe.

I know what you tell me! I am already breathing or I would not be here! Yes of course. The problem is that a majority of people do not know how to breath CORRECTLY.

This is what you need to learn again if you forgot it.

To begin, place your palm on your stomach at the navel. This is necessary to ensure that you breathe through your belly, not just the lungs. I explain in detail the importance of breathing in the audio courses
http://attractitude.us/

Most people breathe through their lungs moving their rib cage. The best way to breathe is to fill its body of air, breathe up to the belly, to the solar plexus.

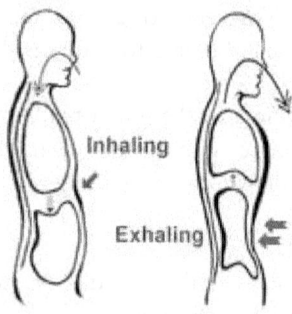

How should we breathe? When you breathe from your belly, you may feel it swell. Women generally like least this way of breathing, as they often seek at all costs to hide their belly. Do it then when no one is watching.

The benefits to healthy breathing through the belly are, among others:

Live a longer and healthier life.
Reduces stress and anxiety
Help fight fear
Help you digest better and offer you more energy, a better supply of oxygen to your cells.
Some doctors even suggest that stress is the cause of belly fat, breathing can significantly help to reduce it.

Try it now. Smile showing your teeth and think of a beautiful day. Take a deep breath down to your abdomen. Practice. If your tummy is tense, you will need several days to clear the nodes of the abdomen. But once that air flows well, you will feel better and better. You can also lie on your back and massage the abdomen in a clockwise direction. This will help your digestion and relaxation.

I want you to breathe consciously bringing air into your belly at least 3 times a day. If you do it more often, it is even better. If you are stressed, breathe. If you are afraid of not being able to pay your bills, breathe. The more you take time to breathe the more you will feel better. Unless you do a sport that requires cardio (like running, aerobics ...), in which case it is recommended to breathe with your lungs. Eventually, you will get into the habit of breathing with the belly.

The more you control your breathing, the more you control your emotions, and emotions are the basis for the positive use of the law of attraction.

If you already know how to breathe, I invite you to take the next step.

Start by emptying all the air from your lungs. Breathe through your nose for four seconds. Keep the air in your stomach for 7 seconds. Then exhale slowly through your mouth for 8 seconds. Do not do this exercise at the wheel of a car because you may experience some dizziness. I suggest you do this exercise a few times a day, every hour if possible. You will be more calm and relaxed, in control of your emotions.

So, are you ready to tackle your second week? Breathing and storing, cleaning. Not very complicated, right?

We can do it !! Are you ready?

Say YES
Say YES
Say YES !!!!!

I can do it
I can do it
I WILL DO IT !!!

I know you can do it. I trust in you!
And I love you!

Take time to note any changes that occur in your habits. Continue to note any signs of abundance (and expenses) around you. Follow the schedule indicated.

Write the date before each day

Day 8: _____
Exercise " I love myself " in front of the mirror in the morning
Visualize for 10-15 minutes

Below is to serve as a diary of all signs of abundance you see.

Morning breathing exercise for one minute

_____
_____
_____
_____
_____
_____

Lunch breathing exercise for one minute

_____
_____
_____
_____
_____
_____
_____
_____
_____

Supper breathing exercise for one minute

_____
_____
_____
_____
_____
_____

Evening: Cleaning and storing

Write the date before each day

Day 9: _____

Exercise " I love myself " in front of the mirror in the morning

Visualize for 10-15 minutes

Below is to serve as a diary of all signs of abundance you see.

Morning breathing exercise for one minute

_____
_____
_____
_____
_____
_____

Lunch breathing exercise for one minute

_____

_____
_____
_____
_____
_____
_____
_____
_____

Supper breathing exercise for one minute

_____
_____
_____
_____
_____
_____

Evening: Cleaning and storing

Write the date before each day

Day 10: _____

Exercise " I love myself " in front of the mirror in the morning

Visualize for 10-15 minutes

Below is to serve as a diary of all signs of abundance you see.

Morning breathing exercise for one minute

_____
_____
_____
_____
_____

Lunch breathing exercise for one minute

_____
_____

_____
_____
_____
_____
_____
_____
_____

Supper breathing exercise for one minute

_____
_____
_____
_____
_____

Evening: Cleaning and storing

Write the date before each day

Day 11: _____
Exercise " I love myself " in front of the mirror in the morning
Visualize for 10-15 minutes

Below is to serve as a diary of all signs of abundance you see.

Morning breathing exercise for one minute

_____
_____
_____
_____
_____

Lunch breathing exercise for one minute

_____
_____
_____

_____
_____
_____
_____
_____
_____

Supper breathing exercise for one minute

_____
_____
_____
_____
_____
_____

Evening: Cleaning and storing

Write the date before each day

Day 12: _____

Exercise " I love myself " in front of the mirror in the morning

Visualize for 10-15 minutes

Below is to serve as a diary of all signs of abundance you see.

Morning breathing exercise for one minute

_____
_____
_____
_____
_____
_____

Lunch breathing exercise for one minute

_____
_____
_____
_____

_____
_____
_____
_____
_____

Supper breathing exercise for one minute

_____
_____
_____
_____
_____
_____

Evening: Cleaning and storing

Write the date before each day

Day 13: _____

Exercise " I love myself " in front of the mirror in the morning

Visualize for 10-15 minutes

Below is to serve as a diary of all signs of abundance you see.

Morning breathing exercise for one minute

_____
_____
_____
_____
_____

Lunch breathing exercise for one minute

_____
_____
_____
_____
_____

_____
_____
_____
_____

Supper breathing exercise for one minute

_____
_____
_____
_____
_____
_____

Evening: Cleaning and storing

Write the date before each day

Day 14: _____

Exercise " I love myself " in front of the mirror in the morning

Visualize for 10-15 minutes

Below is to serve as a diary of all signs of abundance you see.

Morning breathing exercise for one minute

_____
_____
_____
_____
_____
_____

Lunch breathing exercise for one minute

_____
_____
_____
_____
_____
_____

_____
_____
_____

Supper breathing exercise for one minute

_____
_____
_____
_____
_____
_____

Evening: Cleaning and storing

Congratulations, you have completed your second week towards your success!
How do you feel? How is your storage habit? Easy, not so easy?

I know you can do it! I know you'll improve with time!
Do not worry if you forgot to breathe from time to time. The important thing is that you record your mistakes, to improve yourself and to remind you of the distance performed when you reach your goal! You will laugh when you're rich!

Remember: You're awesome!
You're OK!
You are EXTRA!
You are ENOUGH!

How do you feel:

_____
_____
_____
_____
_____
_____
_____

_____
_____
_____
_____
_____
_____
_____
_____
_____
_____
_____

Remember, this will go better and better.
It is only the second week. We take our time so that the results are sustainable.
Do not worry if you missed a day. You are strong, you will catch up.

Before you go on to the next week, I'll explain the next exercise. You will do this at the beginning or end of each day.
The exercise is called 'learning wealth'

Every day, you'll spend an hour reading and studying wealth. You will use the Internet to find the biographies of the rich. You will educate yourself on what made them wealthy. You will live their lives an hour a day.

Most people can't achieve wealth because they simply do not know how. There are many wealthy people who have written on the subject. Many of them had to overcome many obstacles before managing to achieve that status.

The more you read about these people, the more you will learn how they did it, the more you earn mental tools to overcome your own obstacles, you get inspired, motivated and reach your first goal.

You do not need to spend money to get these books. Go to your local library and borrow books that suit you. You can also listen to these stories in your car on your way to work or rent movies that talk about successful people.

There are thousands. The more you learn from others wealth, the more you will see how much it is within your reach.

Furthermore, I would appreciate if every week you take the time to brainstorm all the ways in which you could make more money. At first, you will perhaps not have many ideas. For one hour a week (more if possible) to just ask yourself what you could do to earn more.

I suggest you reread your goal early morning to know exactly how much money you want to receive and then let your imagination flow. Write whatever comes into your mind without judging. Each month, review the list and see if there is an idea that appeals to you more. If this is the case, put it into action!

_____
_____
_____
_____
_____
_____
_____
_____
_____
_____
_____
_____
_____
_____
_____
_____
_____

_____
_____
_____
_____
_____
_____
_____
_____

Write the date before each day

Day 15: _____

Exercise " I love myself " in front of the mirror in the morning

Visualize for 10-15 minutes

Below is to serve as a diary of all signs of abundance you see.

Morning breathing exercise for one minute

_____
_____
_____
_____
_____

Lunch breathing exercise for one minute

_____
_____
_____
_____
_____
_____
_____
_____

Supper breathing exercise for one minute

_____

_____
_____
_____
_____
_____

Evening: Cleaning and storing

Write the date before each day

Day 16: _____
Exercise " I love myself " in front of the mirror in the morning
Visualize for 10-15 minutes

Below is to serve as a diary of all signs of abundance you see.

Morning breathing exercise for one minute

_____
_____
_____
_____
_____
_____

Lunch breathing exercise for one minute

_____
_____
_____
_____
_____
_____
_____
_____

Supper breathing exercise for one minute

_____
_____

_____
_____
_____
_____

Evening: Cleaning and storing

Write the date before each day

Day 17: _____
Exercise " I love myself " in front of the mirror in the morning
Visualize for 10-15 minutes

Below is to serve as a diary of all signs of abundance you see.

Morning breathing exercise for one minute

_____
_____
_____
_____
_____

Lunch breathing exercise for one minute

_____
_____
_____
_____
_____
_____
_____
_____

Supper breathing exercise for one minute

_____
_____
_____

_____
_____
_____

Evening: Cleaning and storing

Write the date before each day

Day 18: _____
Exercise " I love myself " in front of the mirror in the morning
Visualize for 10-15 minutes

Below is to serve as a diary of all signs of abundance you see.

Morning breathing exercise for one minute

_____
_____
_____
_____
_____
_____

Lunch breathing exercise for one minute

_____
_____
_____
_____
_____
_____
_____
_____

Supper breathing exercise for one minute

_____
_____
_____
_____

_____

_____

Evening: Cleaning and storing

Write the date before each day

Day 19: _____

Exercise " I love myself " in front of the mirror in the morning

Visualize for 10-15 minutes

Below is to serve as a diary of all signs of abundance you see.

Morning breathing exercise for one minute

_____

_____

_____

_____

_____

Lunch breathing exercise for one minute

_____

_____

_____

_____

_____

_____

_____

_____

Supper breathing exercise for one minute

_____

_____

_____

_____

_____

Evening: Cleaning and storing

Write the date before each day

Day 20: _____

Exercise " I love myself " in front of the mirror in the morning

Visualize for 10-15 minutes

Below is to serve as a diary of all signs of abundance you see.

Morning breathing exercise for one minute

_____
_____
_____
_____
_____
_____

Lunch breathing exercise for one minute

_____
_____
_____
_____
_____
_____
_____
_____
_____

Supper breathing exercise for one minute

_____
_____
_____
_____
_____
_____

Evening: Cleaning and storing

Write the date before each day

Day 21: _____
Exercise " I love myself " in front of the mirror in the morning
Visualize for 10-15 minutes

Below is to serve as a diary of all signs of abundance you see.

Morning breathing exercise for one minute

_____
_____
_____
_____
_____
_____

Lunch breathing exercise for one minute

_____
_____
_____
_____
_____
_____
_____
_____

Supper breathing exercise for one minute

_____
_____
_____
_____
_____

Evening: Cleaning and storing

Exercise of wealthy thinking and brainstorming. All ideas that can lead to your financial success:

_____

_____

_____

_____

_____

_____

_____

_____

_____

_____

_____

_____

_____

_____

_____

_____

_____

_____

_____

_____

_____

_____

_____

_____

_____

_____

_____

_____

_____

_____

_____

Wow !! You have already completed your 3rd week. Congratulations!

Do you feel proud? How do you feel? Feel your self esteem grow a little more each day! Do you notice more rich people or abundance around you?

I remind you that one of the most important exercises that I asked you to do is first one during which you say 'I love you". Never stop. From now on, you will add another 30 seconds of self love.

Remember. You have to look yourself deep in the eyes and focus on all the love you can feel for yourself, for your soul, for the little kid in you who is asking to be loved again.

Say YES !!!

Write below what can be improved:

_____
_____
_____
_____
_____
_____
_____
_____
_____
_____
_____
_____
_____
_____

This week, which commemorates the first third of your

road to success, you will add two things.

The first is an exercise called: affirmation. You need a piece of paper that you carry with you at all times.

Starting today, you will choose a powerful affirmation that you will repeat 300 times a day. 300 Yes !!
Here are some examples:

Everything is better and better and better
I live in abundance and wealth
All my needs are met and I feel good
I am happy to have more money than I need
Money comes to me easily and quickly
I'm doing a job I love and am well paid

Choose a phrase or create one to your own. You can change from week to week.

When you feel doubt about your success, read this sentence.

I mean it when I say 300 repetitions per day. I explain why in detail in the audios on http://attractitude.us. You repeated enough negative sentences for many years, probably more than 300 times a day. You must change your thinking.

You want to win, right? Here's a great way to get there.

You can choose to distribute your affirmations on a basis of 3 times a day, 100 times every time. You will need to repeat the affirmation until it becomes part of your thought pattern.

Choose an affirmation and write it here:
_____

The second exercise will be called 'wealth accumulation'. It will allow you to change your energy toward a positive state. This week, you will spend $1000 in a fake way (on paper only by listng all the things you buy with that excess of money). You must spend this amount in full.

Here's a great time to read the reasons why you want to become rich.

We can do it !! Are you ready?

Say YES
Say YES
Say YES !!!!!

I can do it
I can do it
I WILL DO IT !!!

Persevere !!!

I LOVE YOU!

Write the date before each day

Day 22: _____

Exercise " I love myself " in front of the mirror in the morning
Visualize for 10-15 minutes
Imagine spending $1000
Repeat your 300 affirmations

Below is to serve as a diary of all signs of abundance you see.

Morning breathing exercise for one minute

_____
_____
_____
_____
_____

Lunch breathing exercise for one minute

_____
_____
_____
_____
_____
_____
_____
_____
_____

Supper breathing exercise for one minute

_____
_____
_____
_____
_____
_____

Evening: Cleaning and storing
Write the date before each day

Day 23: _____
Exercise " I love myself " in front of the mirror in the

morning
Visualize for 10-15 minutes
Imagine spending $1000
Repeat your 300 affirmations

Below is to serve as a diary of all signs of abundance you see.

Morning breathing exercise for one minute

_____
_____
_____
_____
_____

Lunch breathing exercise for one minute

_____
_____
_____
_____
_____
_____
_____
_____

Supper breathing exercise for one minute

_____
_____
_____
_____
_____
_____

Evening: Cleaning and storing
Write the date before each day

Day 24: _____
Exercise " I love myself " in front of the mirror in the morning

Visualize for 10-15 minutes
Imagine spending $1000
Repeat your 300 affirmations

Below is to serve as a diary of all signs of abundance you see.

Morning breathing exercise for one minute

_____
_____
_____
_____
_____

Lunch breathing exercise for one minute

_____
_____
_____
_____
_____
_____
_____
_____

Supper breathing exercise for one minute

_____
_____
_____
_____
_____

Evening: Cleaning and storing
Write the date before each day

Day 25: _____
Exercise " I love myself " in front of the mirror in the morning
Visualize for 10-15 minutes

Imagine spending $1000
Repeat your 300 affirmations

Below is to serve as a diary of all signs of abundance you see.

Morning breathing exercise for one minute

_____
_____
_____
_____
_____

Lunch breathing exercise for one minute

_____
_____
_____
_____
_____
_____
_____
_____

Supper breathing exercise for one minute

_____
_____
_____
_____
_____

Evening: Cleaning and storing
Write the date before each day

Day 26: _____

Exercise " I love myself " in front of the mirror in the morning
Visualize for 10-15 minutes
Imagine spending $1000

Repeat your 300 affirmations

Below is to serve as a diary of all signs of abundance you see.

Morning breathing exercise for one minute

_____
_____
_____
_____
_____

Lunch breathing exercise for one minute

_____
_____
_____
_____
_____
_____
_____
_____

Supper breathing exercise for one minute

_____
_____
_____
_____
_____

Evening: Cleaning and storing
Write the date before each day

Day 27: _____
Exercise " I love myself " in front of the mirror in the morning
Visualize for 10-15 minutes
Imagine spending $1000
Repeat your 300 affirmations

Below is to serve as a diary of all signs of abundance you see.

Morning breathing exercise for one minute

_____
_____
_____
_____
_____

Lunch breathing exercise for one minute

_____
_____
_____
_____
_____
_____
_____
_____

Supper breathing exercise for one minute

_____
_____
_____
_____
_____
_____

Evening: Cleaning and storing
Write the date before each day

Day 28: _____
Exercise " I love myself " in front of the mirror in the morning
Visualize for 10-15 minutes
Imagine spending $1000
Repeat your 300 affirmations

Below is to serve as a diary of all signs of abundance you see.

Morning breathing exercise for one minute

_____
_____
_____
_____
_____

Lunch breathing exercise for one minute

_____
_____
_____
_____
_____
_____
_____
_____
_____

Supper breathing exercise for one minute

_____
_____
_____
_____
_____

Evening: Cleaning and storing
How do you feel?
Here's your first completed month.
CONGRATULATIONS !!!

You must celebrate! Jumping up and down or go for a massage.

I'm really proud of you!

You do all the exercises, you clean your home and you

breathe? You love yourself in the morning and read stories of wealthy people? You repeat your affirmations every day?

Give it your best! Come On !! Tell me that you want to live your life better! You bought this book to get there then you need to invest a little more willpower! I know you can do it! I did it, you can do it too!

Well, you skipped once or twice. It does not matter, you will catch up! I love you!

Become better and better every time! Learn from your mistakes. Identify times when you almost did it and refuse to go back to old patterns of thoughts or habits. Say NO! I love myself too much. Stay the course!

Before we go on, I would like you to calculate all your expenses from last month and that you put them in the following categories :

Necessities	Debt	Fun	Other

I would like you to calculate the percentage that each category represents of your net pay.

Have you noticed if the category " fun " is worth more than 10%.
Observe the proportion of the category 'other'. It includes a lot of gifts to your children?

By becoming more aware of your expenses, you'll be able to subsequently reduce your spending.

Promise yourself not to spend so much. Each coffee, each small meal at the restaurant, every little expenditure accumulates.

Yes, you-have to tighten your belt for a while. The money will be attracted to your by your ability to manage it, respect it(do not waste) and save it.

Starting next month, if you have not started already, I suggest you increase the amount you save (your golden goose) to 10% of your income.

Continue to take into account your expenses.

For week number 5, here's what I want you to do. Two new things.

The first is called gratitude.

Gratitude is very powerful. The more you feel gratitude the more magic shows up in your life. The result will be a more harmonious life and your soul will be filled with happiness. You will feel also much more abundance, which will attract more of it.

What I want you to do is very simple. I want you to get a notebook and write every day 10 things for which you feel gratitude.

For example, you may be grateful to be healthy, because health keeps you alive and allows you to be in the company of those you love.
You can feel gratitude for your job because it offers you money to spend. You can feel gratitude for your family because they love you.

You can also decide to focus only on the energy of gratitude felt in money. For example, to be happy for all the money received in your life. You can choose to appreciate past expenditures and even feel gratitude for the money to come.

You get the idea? Place the notebook near your bed before you go to bed, write down the reasons for your gratitude. 10 things at least. It's very simple. You will realize that you will sleep better. Eventually, you will be in a better mood. You will wake up with gratitude.

The second thing I'd like you to do is to write yourself a promise. It sounds strange, but it is very important. Why? Because we love to write our vows and promises to the people we love, so why not start with us?

You will write yourself a solemn pledge below. For example, you must promise that you will always have a good sleep, never eat more than you need, develop compassion towards yourself and love yourself...

Write it in your own words and copy it on a piece of paper.

_____

_____

_____

_____

_____

_____

I want you to read this promise every day in the middle of the day, like a prayer. A promise of your love for you, simply said.

This exercise is important (like any other), because it will increase your appreciation of yourself and your own love. You never want to hurt someone you love so you're going to love yourself infinitely. The more you are going to put the focus on love, the more you will attract good things to you. The more you love yourself, the less you accept drama in your life. These will make up to prosperity. The happiness felt by increasing love will help you attract wealth. Remember, a person who loves oneself cannot sabotage ones self.

Joy, love, happiness attracts money and you need to develop those feelings deep within you.

We can do it !! Are you ready?

say YES
say YES
Say YES !!!!!

I can do it

I can do it
I WILL DO IT !!!

Write the date before each day

Day 29: _____

Exercise " I love myself " in front of the mirror in the morning

Visualize for 10-15 minutes

Imagine spending $3000 (increase this amount)

Repeat your 300 affirmations

Below is to serve as a diary of all signs of abundance you see.

Morning breathing exercise for one minute

_____
_____
_____
_____
_____

Lunch breathing exercise for one minute
Your promise and prayer

_____
_____
_____
_____
_____
_____
_____

Supper breathing exercise for one minute

_____
_____
_____
_____
_____Eveni
ng: Cleaning and storing
10 reasons for feeling grateful

Write the date before each day

Day 30: _____
Exercise " I love myself " in front of the mirror in the
morning
Visualize for 10-15 minutes
Imagine spending $3000
Repeat your 300 affirmations

Below is to serve as a diary of all signs of abundance
you see.

Morning breathing exercise for one minute

_____
_____
_____
_____
_____

Lunch breathing exercise for one minute
Your promise and prayer

_____
_____
_____
_____
_____
_____
_____

Supper breathing exercise for one minute

_____
_____
_____
_____
_____Eveni
ng: Cleaning and storing
10 reasons for feeling grateful

Write the date before each day

Day 31: _____
Exercise " I love myself " in front of the mirror in the morning
Visualize for 10-15 minutes
Imagine spending $3000
Repeat your 300 affirmations

Below is to serve as a diary of all signs of abundance you see.

Morning breathing exercise for one minute

_____
_____
_____
_____
_____

Lunch breathing exercise for one minute
Your promise and prayer

_____
_____
_____
_____
_____
_____
_____

Supper breathing exercise for one minute

_____
_____
_____
_____
_____Eveni

ng: Cleaning and storing
10 reasons for feeling grateful

Write the date before each day

Day 32: _____
Exercise " I love myself " in front of the mirror in the morning
Visualize for 10-15 minutes
Imagine spending $3000
Repeat your 300 affirmations

Below is to serve as a diary of all signs of abundance you see.

Morning breathing exercise for one minute

_____
_____
_____
_____

Lunch breathing exercise for one minute
Your promise and prayer

_____
_____
_____
_____
_____
_____

Supper breathing exercise for one minute

_____
_____
_____
_____Eveni
ng: Cleaning and storing
10 reasons for feeling grateful

Write the date before each day

Day 33: _____
Exercise " I love myself " in front of the mirror in the
morning
Visualize for 10-15 minutes
Imagine spending $3000
Repeat your 300 affirmations

Below is to serve as a diary of all signs of abundance
you see.

Morning breathing exercise for one minute

_____

_____

_____

_____

_____

Lunch breathing exercise for one minute
Your promise and prayer

_____

_____

_____

_____

_____

_____

_____

Supper breathing exercise for one minute

_____

_____

_____

_____Eveni

ng: Cleaning and storing
10 reasons for feeling grateful

Write the date before each day

Day 34: _____
Exercise " I love myself " in front of the mirror in the
morning
Visualize for 10-15 minutes
Imagine spending $3000
Repeat your 300 affirmations

Below is to serve as a diary of all signs of abundance
you see.

Morning breathing exercise for one minute

_____
_____
_____
_____
_____

Lunch breathing exercise for one minute
Your promise and prayer

_____
_____
_____
_____
_____
_____
_____

Supper breathing exercise for one minute

_____
_____
_____
_____
_____Eveni
ng: Cleaning and storing
10 reasons for feeling grateful

Write the date before each day

Day 35: _____
Exercise " I love myself " in front of the mirror in the morning
Visualize for 10-15 minutes
Imagine spending $3000
Repeat your 300 affirmations

Below is to serve as a diary of all signs of abundance you see.

Morning breathing exercise for one minute

_____
_____
_____
_____
_____

Lunch breathing exercise for one minute
Your promise and prayer

_____
_____
_____
_____
_____
_____

Supper breathing exercise for one minute

_____
_____
_____
_____Eveni
ng: Cleaning and storing
10 reasons for feeling grateful

Brainstorm. All ideas to get more money in my life:

_____
_____
_____
_____
_____
_____
_____
_____
_____
_____
_____
_____

How do you feel?

I'm sure you feel better about yourself and about your life. If you do everything I tell you, you must receive compliments about how you look different and better!

Otherwise, you do not-have to worry, aim to ask why you do not find the time to do all the exercises. You have to do them. You bought the book, you started off right. You must continue!

Are you still able to virtually spend all the money on paper? No? Then you haven't reached a first threshold of wealth. The more you increase your field of vision and open your mind to the endless possibilities to enrich yourself, the more you'll be able to spend this fake money, until one day soon it becomes real. You can spend it over and over on the same things, that's fine. I just want you to get into the habit of budgeting larger amounts of money.

I know you can do it! I'm sure.

Take the time to look at your situation, the pros and cons. Think about the excuses that prevent you from doing the exercises every day. Do you promise to try harder this following week. Believe in yourself! You have the power! Take it!

_____
_____
_____
_____
_____
_____

This week, you will add one new exercise to your new routine.

It is called silence. Many people speak of the benefits of meditation. Unfortunately, the majority of the population does not use it. If you do, congratulations! Otherwise, here's an example of how to meditate. You can find it in my online course here: http://attractitude.us

If you have never meditated before, you wonder why you should do it. All people who are successful practice meditation. This will help you increase your power of concentration and calm and help you focus on what really matters.

We live in a world that moves a lot in which we lose ourselves often, whether in our work or our relationships. How often do we hear people say, 'I am looking for myself.' ' Too many people live by proxy, to please others. By remaining silent, we can find our deepest essence and nourish our soul. At the same time, you'll slow down your thoughts, allowing you to stop the negative self-talk. Your concentration level will be higher and you may feel calmer and in control of your emotions.

For beginners, I would simply ask you a 5 minute silence to start with and gradually increase your dose up to get 20 minutes of daily silence.

How to find the time? Get up earlier, it's easy. Many people watch television an average of 3-4 hours a day. You can surely find 5 minutes in your day.

There are different ways to meditate. You should get used to meditating twice a day. The one I use most frequently is the simplest.

It is simply to focus your attention on your breathing. Believe me, this is the most difficult thing to do and the simplest. You need to find a quiet place where you will not be disturbed. If you have children, you can lock yourself in the bathroom for some quiet time. Otherwise, ask your spouse to take care of them. You have the right to this moment of tranquility. You will be better able to offer more love if you do so.

Find a comfortable seat and sit with your hands flat

on your lap with palms facing the sky. Both feet should be properly anchored to the ground. Breathe deeply and pay attention to your breathing. Close your eyes and calm down.

Note the cooler air coming in and the one who comes out hotter. Consider that you clean your body with each breath. Let your mind rest and relax. You have many thoughts going around in your head and it is necessary to empty it. Let them pass and pay attention to your breathing. Do not pay attention to your thoughts. There will be many at first, then less and less. With time, you will have more silent and almost no intrusive thoughts.

Another way to do this is to make a list of everything you want (outline). Read the list out loud and imagine having everything already obtained. How would you feel? Relieved? Take a deep breath, release your breath and relax! Imagine that you have achieved all your goals. Adopt the feeling of relief. Get used to the feeling.
We can do it !! Are you ready?

Say YES
Say YES
Say YES !!!!!

I can do it
I can do it
I WILL DO IT !!!

Write the date before each day

Day 36: _____

Exercise " I love myself " in front of the mirror in the morning for at least 2 minutes

Silence for at least 5 minutes

Visualize for 10-15 minutes

Imagine spending $3000

Repeat your 300 affirmations

Below is to serve as a diary of all signs of abundance you see.

Morning breathing exercise for one minute

_____
_____
_____
_____
_____

Lunch breathing exercise for one minute
Your promise and prayer

_____
_____
_____
_____
_____
_____
_____

Supper breathing exercise for one minute

_____
_____
_____
_____
_____Eveni

ng: Cleaning and storing
10 reasons for feeling grateful
Write the date before each day

Day 37: _____
Exercise " I love myself " in front of the mirror in the
morning for at least 2 minutes
Silence for at least 5 minutes
Visualize for 10-15 minutes
Imagine spending $3000
Repeat your 300 affirmations

Below is to serve as a diary of all signs of abundance
you see.

Morning breathing exercise for one minute

_____
_____
_____
_____
_____

Lunch breathing exercise for one minute

Your promise and prayer

_____
_____
_____
_____
_____
_____
_____

Supper breathing exercise for one minute

_____
_____
_____
_____
_____Eveni
ng: Cleaning and storing
10 reasons for feeling grateful
Write the date before each day

Day 38: _____
Exercise " I love myself " in front of the mirror in the morning for at least 2 minutes
Silence for at least 5 minutes
Visualize for 10-15 minutes
Imagine spending $3000
Repeat your 300 affirmations

Below is to serve as a diary of all signs of abundance you see.

Morning breathing exercise for one minute

_____
_____
_____
_____

Lunch breathing exercise for one minute
Your promise and prayer

_____

_____

_____

_____

_____

_____

_____

Supper breathing exercise for one minute

_____

_____

_____

_____Eveni

ng: Cleaning and storing
10 reasons for feeling grateful
Write the date before each day

Day 39: _____

Exercise " I love myself " in front of the mirror in the
morning for at least 2 minutes
Silence for at least 5 minutes
Visualize for 10-15 minutes
Imagine spending $3000
Repeat your 300 affirmations

Below is to serve as a diary of all signs of abundance
you see.

Morning breathing exercise for one minute

_____

_____

_____

_____

_____

Lunch breathing exercise for one minute
Your promise and prayer

_____

_____
_____
_____
_____
_____
_____

Supper breathing exercise for one minute

_____
_____
_____
_____
_____Eveni

ng: Cleaning and storing
10 reasons for feeling grateful
Write the date before each day

Day 40: _____
Exercise " I love myself " in front of the mirror in the morning for at least 2 minutes
Silence for at least 5 minutes
Visualize for 10-15 minutes
Imagine spending $3000
Repeat your 300 affirmations

Below is to serve as a diary of all signs of abundance you see.

Morning breathing exercise for one minute

_____
_____
_____
_____
_____

Lunch breathing exercise for one minute
Your promise and prayer

_____
_____

_____

_____

_____

_____

_____

Supper breathing exercise for one minute

_____

_____

_____

_____Eveni

ng: Cleaning and storing
10 reasons for feeling grateful
Write the date before each day

Day 41: _____

Exercise " I love myself " in front of the mirror in the morning for at least 2 minutes

Silence for at least 5 minutes

Visualize for 10-15 minutes

Imagine spending $3000

Repeat your 300 affirmations

Below is to serve as a diary of all signs of abundance you see.

Morning breathing exercise for one minute

_____

_____

_____

_____

_____

Lunch breathing exercise for one minute
Your promise and prayer

_____

_____

_____

_____
_____
_____
_____

Supper breathing exercise for one minute

_____
_____
_____
_____ Eveni
ng: Cleaning and storing
10 reasons for feeling grateful
That's it! You're halfway through the program!
CONGRATULATIONS!
You've made it!
Applaud yourself loud and clear!
Celebrate by cooking yourself a nice meal!

YES, YOU WILL GET THERE!

How did you feel in the silence? Did you feel a lot
of thoughts bothering you, prevented you to stay
quiet. This is normal. With time, you will have
fewer obsessive and negative thoughts.

You do not have to fear silence. Instead, you will do
much better with time. Do not be afraid. Nothing
bad can happen to you. If you have bad memories
that resurface, you can let them pass without
reliving them and without judging them. Everyone
has negative thoughts that resurface. With time, you
will learn to let them be and not be bothered by the
past. Leave it where it belongs: in the past.

Enter below the times when you couldn't do it, fears

you have and promise to do better:

_____

_____

_____

_____

_____

_____

_____

_____

_____

For week 7, we will get a little more serious. We'll go up to the next level.

You will add light exercise to your routine. YES !! You have to move! For those who already move a lot, you can add yoga, for example, or more sports.

I want you to do what you have often postponed.

Write what exercise you promise you to:

_____

This week, you'll have more results for your body and for your mind. Remember that you love yourself and, therefore, you want to show yourself that love. In addition, the law of attraction requires a higher frequency energy. Sports allow you to increase this positive frequency. In addition, it puts you in a good mood and cheerfulness is a sign that your life is better. Through the law of attraction, you therefore attract better circumstances.

The more you pay attention to your well-being and your body the more you will attract good things into your life, in every aspect of it.

I want you to take the time to start at least one activity that relates to what you love to do, that fills you with joy.

Many people want to have more money to have more time to do what they love to do. You can now practice some activities you most enjoy in smaller doses until you are able to pay for more.

Do not wait to be rich or retired to live with passion. First, fully live your life and wealth will come to you. Take your calendar and block your schedule to get started quickly. Do not worry, everyone is like you. Everyone is afraid of starting something new. No worries.

Moreover, from now, if this is not already the case, I want you to monitor your diet. Too much coffee, sugar, alcohol or other poisons, hearty dishes are lowering your energy state. You will increase your water consumption.

I want you to spend more time listening to inspiring music. Go dancing, have fun, relearn to laugh more often. Don't give as much importance to anything that seems too serious.

You must also learn not to worry. If you are used to being worried, anxious of the future, stressed out because of your problems, this state becomes your comfort zone. If you constantly run after success, the quest and not the achieving becomes the norm. As soon as you come out of this " normal " state, you will be outside of your comfort zone and into the unknown. You will have more chances sabotage your success in order to return to the area known as stress and worries.

This is one reason why many people sabotage their success. Success, that feeling of being at the top, and relief can be scary if never experienced. Some individuals will remain in an extremely precarious situation even hostile because they got used to it.

To greatly improve your living conditions and achieve your dreams, you have to now become accustomed to living in success. To do this, you must practice to stop accepting stress and worry as your choices of reactions. It is necessary to act in every area of his life by paying attention to this, shifting your feelings, taking your time, living successfully.

Visualize how you behave when you have achieved your dreams and not worry about anything. You could finally take the time to live and enjoy your life fully. It's that feeling that you need to develop now. Take five minutes a day to soak up the feeling of well-being and relief.

It is essential that your comfort zone becomes relief, joy, serenity. This may be hard to imagine, but it can be learned. Over the years, you've practiced for hours, the art of worry and stress.

If your central point, your anchor, your center of gravity are the concerns about lack, you will not be able to change your state of being rapidly and move away without experiencing an imbalance. The concern and stress feelings are choices that you can change.

In most cases, they are associated with future contingencies which are not really grounded in the present, but are mistakenly based on more or less similar experiences in the past. Learn therefore to choose the feeling of relaxation and not of concern and you will attract the circumstances that allow that feeling to grow.

We can do it !! Are you ready?

Say YES
Say YES
Say YES !!!!!

I can do it
I can do it
I WILL DO IT !!!

Write the date before each day

Day 42: _____

Exercise " I love myself " in front of the mirror in the morning for at least 2 minutes

Silence for at least 5 minutes

Visualize for 10-15 minutes

Imagine spending $3000

Repeat your 300 affirmations

Below is to serve as a diary of all signs of abundance you see.

Morning breathing exercise for one minute

_____
_____
_____
_____
_____

Lunch breathing exercise for one minute
Your promise and prayer

_____
_____
_____
_____
_____
_____
_____

Supper breathing exercise for one minute

_____
_____
_____
_____Eve
ning: Cleaning and storing
Light exercise like yoga or a brisk walk
10 reasons for feeling grateful
Write the date before each day

Day 43: _____
Exercise " I love myself " in front of the mirror in the
morning for at least 2 minutes
Silence for at least 5 minutes
Visualize for 10-15 minutes
Imagine spending $3000
Repeat your 300 affirmations

Below is to serve as a diary of all signs of abundance
you see.

Morning breathing exercise for one minute

_____
_____
_____
_____
_____

Lunch breathing exercise for one minute
Your promise and prayer

_____
_____
_____
_____
_____
_____
_____

Supper breathing exercise for one minute

_____

_____

_____

_____Eve

ning: Cleaning and storing
Light exercise like yoga or a brisk walk
10 reasons for feeling grateful
Write the date before each day

    Day 44: _____
    Exercise " I love myself " in front of the mirror in the
morning for at least 2 minutes
    Silence for at least 5 minutes
    Visualize for 10-15 minutes
    Imagine spending $3000
    Repeat your 300 affirmations

    Below is to serve as a diary of all signs of abundance
you see.

 Morning breathing exercise for one minute

_____

_____

_____

_____

_____

Lunch breathing exercise for one minute
Your promise and prayer

_____

_____

_____

_____

_____

_____

_____

Supper breathing exercise for one minute

_____
_____
_____
_____Eve
ning: Cleaning and storing
Light exercise like yoga or a brisk walk
10 reasons for feeling grateful
Write the date before each day

Day 45: _____
Exercise " I love myself " in front of the mirror in the
morning for at least 2 minutes
Silence for at least 5 minutes
Visualize for 10-15 minutes
Imagine spending $3000
Repeat your 300 affirmations

Below is to serve as a diary of all signs of abundance
you see.

Morning breathing exercise for one minute

_____
_____
_____
_____
_____

Lunch breathing exercise for one minute
Your promise and prayer

_____
_____
_____
_____
_____
_____
_____

Supper breathing exercise for one minute

_____
_____
_____
_____Eve
ning: Cleaning and storing
Light exercise like yoga or a brisk walk
10 reasons for feeling grateful
Write the date before each day

Day 46: _____
Exercise " I love myself " in front of the mirror in the
morning for at least 2 minutes
Silence for at least 5 minutes
Visualize for 10-15 minutes
Imagine spending $3000
Repeat your 300 affirmations

Below is to serve as a diary of all signs of abundance
you see.

Morning breathing exercise for one minute

_____
_____
_____
_____
_____

Lunch breathing exercise for one minute
Your promise and prayer

_____
_____
_____
_____
_____
_____
_____

Supper breathing exercise for one minute

_____
_____
_____
_____Eve
ning: Cleaning and storing
Light exercise like yoga or a brisk walk
10 reasons for feeling grateful
Write the date before each day

Day 47: _____
Exercise " I love myself " in front of the mirror in the
morning for at least 2 minutes
Silence for at least 5 minutes
Visualize for 10-15 minutes
Imagine spending $3000
Repeat your 300 affirmations

Below is to serve as a diary of all signs of abundance
you see.

Morning breathing exercise for one minute

_____
_____
_____
_____
_____

Lunch breathing exercise for one minute
Your promise and prayer

_____
_____
_____
_____
_____
_____
_____

Supper breathing exercise for one minute

_____
_____
_____
_____Eve
ning: Cleaning and storing
Light exercise like yoga or a brisk walk
10 reasons for feeling grateful
Write the date before each day

Day 48: _____
Exercise " I love myself " in front of the mirror in the morning for at least 2 minutes
Silence for at least 5 minutes
Visualize for 10-15 minutes
Imagine spending $3000
Repeat your 300 affirmations

Below is to serve as a diary of all signs of abundance you see.

Morning breathing exercise for one minute

_____
_____
_____
_____
_____

Lunch breathing exercise for one minute
Your promise and prayer

_____
_____
_____
_____
_____
_____
_____

Supper breathing exercise for one minute

_____

_____

_____

_____Eve
ning: Cleaning and storing
Light exercise like yoga or a brisk walk
10 reasons for feeling grateful
Brainstorm: All the ideas on how I can create more
money:

_____

_____

_____

_____

_____

_____

_____

_____

_____

_____

_____

_____

_____

_____

_____

_____

_____

_____

_____

_____

_____

_____

_____

_____

_____
_____
_____
_____

_____

OK great. I know. You probably did not do physical exercises at the indicated times. Have you done a bit? Please do not give me the excuse of lack of time.

You know you can find the time. You can mute the TV or social media. It must be, for the love of you!

Read your promise and your reasons for wanting to attract abundance and motivate yourself to take a first step and then a second. You will be even more proud when you get there.

You know I love you. You love yourself. You have to improve yourself and do your best every day to get you where you want to be. You can do that!

Enter below the times when you failed and promise to do better:

_____
_____
_____
_____
_____
_____
_____
_____
_____
_____

_____
_____
_____

For the 8th week, we will add exercise of gratitude upon awakening.

Each morning, you can change your circumstances. You have every day the opportunity to change and improve. No matter what happened the day before, the future may have new opportunities, people and ideas that can help you, new solutions that you had not considered.

As soon as you open your eyes, I want you to think of reasons that make you appreciate life. Take 2-3 minutes before getting up. Several negative thoughts can come up. Deciding to be positive and redirect your thought toward appreciation.

The more you live in gratitude the more you will attract more reasons to enjoy your life. I guarantee it! Your vibration level will be higher and you will create more luck. You will attract more and more positive circumstances.

We can do it !! Are you ready?

Say YES
Say YES
Say YES !!!!!

I can do it
I can do it
I WILL DO IT !!!

Write the date before each day

Wake up in gratitude

Day 49: _____

Exercise " I love myself " in front of the mirror in the morning for at least 2 minutes

Silence for at least 5 minutes

Visualize for 10-15 minutes

Imagine spending $3000

Repeat your 300 affirmations

Below is to serve as a diary of all signs of abundance you see.

Morning breathing exercise for one minute

_____

_____

_____

_Lunch breathing exercise for one minute

Your promise and prayer

_____

_____

_____

_____

_____

_____

_____

Supper breathing exercise for one minute

_____

_____

_____

_____Eve

ning: Cleaning and storing
Light exercise like yoga or a brisk walk
10 reasons for feeling grateful
Write the date before each day

Wake up in gratitude

Day 50: _____
Exercise " I love myself " in front of the mirror in the
morning for at least 2 minutes
Silence for at least 5 minutes
Visualize for 10-15 minutes
Imagine spending $3000
Repeat your 300 affirmations

Below is to serve as a diary of all signs of abundance
you see.

Morning breathing exercise for one minute

_____
_____
_____

_Lunch breathing exercise for one minute
Your promise and prayer

_____
_____
_____
_____
_____
_____
_____

Supper breathing exercise for one minute

_____
_____
_____
_____Eve

ning: Cleaning and storing
Light exercise like yoga or a brisk walk
10 reasons for feeling grateful
Write the date before each day

Wake up in gratitude

Day 51: _____
Exercise " I love myself " in front of the mirror in the morning for at least 2 minutes
Silence for at least 5 minutes
Visualize for 10-15 minutes
Imagine spending $3000
Repeat your 300 affirmations

Below is to serve as a diary of all signs of abundance you see.

Morning breathing exercise for one minute

_____
_____
_____

_Lunch breathing exercise for one minute
Your promise and prayer

_____
_____
_____
_____
_____
_____
_____

Supper breathing exercise for one minute

_____
_____
_____
_____Eve

ning: Cleaning and storing
Light exercise like yoga or a brisk walk
10 reasons for feeling grateful
Write the date before each day

Wake up in gratitude

Day 52: _____
Exercise " I love myself " in front of the mirror in the morning for at least 2 minutes
Silence for at least 5 minutes
Visualize for 10-15 minutes
Imagine spending $3000
Repeat your 300 affirmations

Below is to serve as a diary of all signs of abundance you see.

Morning breathing exercise for one minute

_____
_____
_____

_Lunch breathing exercise for one minute
Your promise and prayer

_____
_____
_____
_____
_____
_____
_____

Supper breathing exercise for one minute

_____
_____
_____
_____Eve

ning: Cleaning and storing
Light exercise like yoga or a brisk walk
10 reasons for feeling grateful
Write the date before each day

Wake up in gratitude

Day 53: _____
Exercise " I love myself " in front of the mirror in the morning for at least 2 minutes
Silence for at least 5 minutes
Visualize for 10-15 minutes
Imagine spending $3000
Repeat your 300 affirmations

Below is to serve as a diary of all signs of abundance you see.

Morning breathing exercise for one minute

_____
_____
_____

_Lunch breathing exercise for one minute
Your promise and prayer

_____
_____
_____
_____
_____
_____

Supper breathing exercise for one minute

_____
_____
_____
_____Eve

ning: Cleaning and storing
Light exercise like yoga or a brisk walk
10 reasons for feeling grateful
Write the date before each day

Wake up in gratitude

Day 54: _____
Exercise " I love myself " in front of the mirror in the
morning for at least 2 minutes
Silence for at least 5 minutes
Visualize for 10-15 minutes
Imagine spending $3000
Repeat your 300 affirmations

Below is to serve as a diary of all signs of abundance
you see.

Morning breathing exercise for one minute

_____
_____
_____

_Lunch breathing exercise for one minute
Your promise and prayer

_____
_____
_____
_____
_____
_____
_____

Supper breathing exercise for one minute

_____
_____
_____
_____Eve

ning: Cleaning and storing
Light exercise like yoga or a brisk walk
10 reasons for feeling grateful
Write the date before each day

Wake up I gratitude

Day 55: _____
Exercise " I love myself " in front of the mirror in the morning for at least 2 minutes
Silence for at least 5 minutes
Visualize for 10-15 minutes
Imagine spending $3000
Repeat your 300 affirmations

Below is to serve as a diary of all signs of abundance you see.

Morning breathing exercise for one minute

_____
_____
_____

Lunch breathing exercise for one minute
Your promise and prayer

_____
_____
_____
_____
_____
_____
_____

Supper breathing exercise for one minute

_____
_____
_____
_____Eve

ning: Cleaning and storing
Light exercise like yoga or a brisk walk
10 reasons for feeling grateful
How do you feel? Have you managed to do all the exercises? Do not feel bad if you have not been able, this happens all the time. Are you ashamed of your behavior? Don't beat yourself up! Do you worry too much? This happens to everyone. You'll do better next time.

Do not blame your family, your children, your spouse or your friends. Take full responsibility of your life. You can't say " no " to people. We must learn to be strong and decide to change. You are able to get your life back and control it 100% when you take 100% responsibility for it..

Remember how good you will feel when you get to your goal! Visualize the results as often as possible! Close your eyes and imagine your happiness when you are rich.

Enter below the times when you missed steps and you promise to do better:

_____

_____

_____

_____

_____

_____

_____

_____

_____

_____

_____

Week 9, we are cleaning your past.

The past is no guarantee of your future circumstances. Often, past experiences, especially if they are negative, will block us from attracting a positive future.

It is important to change this. In the following exercise, you will describe a past event, connected to your financial situation. I would like you to describe the experience in detail. Then you will describe how this experience was needed and helpful in your present and influenced it. What are the negative thoughts associated with it?

First you'll only indicate that the event happened, without adding interpretation. You need to exclude all the emotional elements related to the event expressed.

_____
_____
_____
_____
_____
_____
_____
_____
_____
_____
_____
_____
_____
_____
_____

Secondly, you add how you interpreted this situation. For example, an event can be described as: " I lost my wallet. " Interpretation may be: " I can't handle money, I lose all my money. I can' manage money" Write the way you interpreted this event:

_____
_____
_____
_____
_____
_____
_____
_____
_____
_____
_____
_____
_____

Finally, you will change the interpretation and create a more positive one. For example, I made a bad investment where I lost my money. I interpreted "There is more money in the universe and I gained experience". Interpret these events differently. You will begin by breathing deeply and then exhale, you release a big "SO WHAT".

_____
_____
_____
_____
_____
_____

I would like you to regularly do this exercise. Once you

have a negative thought that comes from the past, I want you clean the event of its negative emotional charge, you look at it without emotion. Then I want you to find the positive side of the situation.

This will completely change your energy level. This will allow you to get rid of negative memories and not to let them influence your future.

The more good you feel good, the more you will be attracting positive circumstances. And the more you will feel good, the more people will act differently around you. It's a wonderful cycle that will take you on a magical life filled with prosperity and happiness.

In addition try to keep away from negative people. Do not watch the news, especially if they talk about economic crisis! Surround yourself with positive images, optimistic one. Continue !! You are on the right track. Do all the exercises.

We can do it !! Are you ready?

Say YES
Say YES
Say YES !!!!!

I can do it
I can do it
I WILL DO IT !!!

Write the date before each day

Wake up in gratitude

Day 56: _____

Exercise " I love myself " in front of the mirror in the morning for at least 2 minutes

Silence for at least 5 minutes

Visualize for 10-15 minutes

Imagine spending $3000

Repeat your 300 affirmations

Below is to serve as a diary of all signs of abundance you see.

Morning breathing exercise for one minute

_____
_____
_____

Lunch breathing exercise for one minute
Your promise and prayer

_____
_____
_____
_____
_____
_____
_____

Supper breathing exercise for one minute

_____
_____
_____
_____Eve
ning: Cleaning and storing
Light exercise like yoga or a brisk walk
10 reasons for feeling grateful
Write the date before each day

Wake up in gratitude

Day 57: _____

Exercise " I love myself " in front of the mirror in the morning for at least 2 minutes

Silence for at least 5 minutes

Visualize for 10-15 minutes

Imagine spending $3000

Repeat your 300 affirmations

Below is to serve as a diary of all signs of abundance you see.

Morning breathing exercise for one minute

_____

_____

_____

Lunch breathing exercise for one minute

Your promise and prayer

_____

_____

_____

_____

_____

_____

_____

Supper breathing exercise for one minute

_____

_____

_____

_____ Eve

ning: Cleaning and storing

Light exercise like yoga or a brisk walk

10 reasons for feeling grateful

Write the date before each day

Wake up in gratitude

Day 58: _____

Exercise " I love myself " in front of the mirror in the morning for at least 2 minutes

Silence for at least 5 minutes

Visualize for 10-15 minutes

Imagine spending $3000

Repeat your 300 affirmations

Below is to serve as a diary of all signs of abundance you see.

Morning breathing exercise for one minute

_____

_____

_____

Lunch breathing exercise for one minute
Your promise and prayer

_____

_____

_____

_____

_____

_____

_____

Supper breathing exercise for one minute

_____

_____

_____

_____Eve

ning: Cleaning and storing

Light exercise like yoga or a brisk walk

10 reasons for feeling grateful

Write the date before each day

Wake up in gratitude

Day 59: _____
Exercise " I love myself " in front of the mirror in the morning for at least 2 minutes
Silence for at least 5 minutes
Visualize for 10-15 minutes
Imagine spending $3000
Repeat your 300 affirmations

Below is to serve as a diary of all signs of abundance you see.

Morning breathing exercise for one minute

_____
_____
_____

Lunch breathing exercise for one minute
Your promise and prayer

_____
_____
_____
_____
_____
_____
_____

Supper breathing exercise for one minute

_____
_____
_____
_____Eve
ning: Cleaning and storing
Light exercise like yoga or a brisk walk
10 reasons for feeling grateful
Write the date before each day

Wake up in gratitude

Day 60: _____

Exercise " I love myself " in front of the mirror in the morning for at least 2 minutes

Silence for at least 5 minutes

Visualize for 10-15 minutes

Imagine spending $3000

Repeat your 300 affirmations

Below is to serve as a diary of all signs of abundance you see.

Morning breathing exercise for one minute

_____

_____

_____

Lunch breathing exercise for one minute
Your promise and prayer

_____

_____

_____

_____

_____

_____

_____

Supper breathing exercise for one minute

_____

_____

_____

_____Eve

ning: Cleaning and storing

Light exercise like yoga or a brisk walk

10 reasons for feeling grateful

Write the date before each day

Wake up in gratitude

Day 61: _____

Exercise " I love myself " in front of the mirror in the morning for at least 2 minutes

Silence for at least 5 minutes

Visualize for 10-15 minutes

Imagine spending $3000

Repeat your 300 affirmations

Below is to serve as a diary of all signs of abundance you see.

Morning breathing exercise for one minute

_____
_____
_____

Lunch breathing exercise for one minute
Your promise and prayer

_____
_____
_____
_____
_____
_____
_____

Supper breathing exercise for one minute

_____
_____
_____
_____Eve

ning: Cleaning and storing

Light exercise like yoga or a brisk walk

10 reasons for feeling grateful

Write the date before each day

Wake up in gratitude

Day 62: _____

Exercise " I love myself " in front of the mirror in the morning for at least 2 minutes

Silence for at least 5 minutes

Visualize for 10-15 minutes

Imagine spending $3000

Repeat your 300 affirmations

Below is to serve as a diary of all signs of abundance you see.

Morning breathing exercise for one minute

_____

_____

_____

Lunch breathing exercise for one minute

Your promise and prayer

_____

_____

_____

_____

_____

_____

_____

Supper breathing exercise for one minute

_____

_____

_____

_____Eve

ning: Cleaning and storing

Light exercise like yoga or a brisk walk

10 reasons for feeling grateful

You passed the second month. If you do all the exercises, you should already see big changes in your financial situation. I would like you to calculate your expenses the previous month and like you to them in the following categories:

Necessities	Debt	Fun	Other

I would like you to calculate what percentage each of these new categories represent of your net pay.

You should be closer to the wanted percentages. You should not have more than 10% of expenses related to fun.

You can always improve.

Continue to pay attention to your daily expenses

Write the date before each day

Wake up in gratitude

Day 63: _____

Exercise " I love myself " in front of the mirror in the morning for at least 2 minutes

Silence for at least 5 minutes

Visualize for 10-15 minutes

Imagine spending $3000

Repeat your 300 affirmations

Below is to serve as a diary of all signs of abundance you see.

Morning breathing exercise for one minute

_____
_____
_____

Lunch breathing exercise for one minute
Your promise and prayer

_____
_____
_____
_____
_____
_____
_____

Supper breathing exercise for one minute

_____
_____
_____
_____Eve

ning: Cleaning and storing

Light exercise like yoga or a brisk walk

10 reasons for feeling grateful

Write the date before each day

Wake up in gratitude

Day 64: _____

Exercise " I love myself " in front of the mirror in the morning for at least 2 minutes
Silence for at least 5 minutes
Visualize for 10-15 minutes
Imagine spending $3000
Repeat your 300 affirmations

Below is to serve as a diary of all signs of abundance you see.

Morning breathing exercise for one minute

_____
_____
_____

Lunch breathing exercise for one minute
Your promise and prayer

_____
_____
_____
_____
_____
_____
_____

Supper breathing exercise for one minute

_____
_____
_____
_____Eve

ning: Cleaning and storing
Light exercise like yoga or a brisk walk
10 reasons for feeling grateful
Write the date before each day

Wake up in gratitude

Day 65: _____

Exercise " I love myself " in front of the mirror in the morning for at least 2 minutes

Silence for at least 5 minutes

Visualize for 10-15 minutes

Imagine spending $3000

Repeat your 300 affirmations

Below is to serve as a diary of all signs of abundance you see.

Morning breathing exercise for one minute

_____

_____

_____

Lunch breathing exercise for one minute

Your promise and prayer

_____

_____

_____

_____

_____

_____

_____

Supper breathing exercise for one minute

_____

_____

_____

_____Eve

ning: Cleaning and storing

Light exercise like yoga or a brisk walk

10 reasons for feeling grateful

Write the date before each day

Wake up in gratitude

Day 66: _____

Exercise " I love myself " in front of the mirror in the morning for at least 2 minutes

Silence for at least 5 minutes

Visualize for 10-15 minutes

Imagine spending $3000

Repeat your 300 affirmations

Below is to serve as a diary of all signs of abundance you see.

Morning breathing exercise for one minute

_____
_____
_____

Lunch breathing exercise for one minute
Your promise and prayer

_____
_____
_____
_____
_____
_____
_____

Supper breathing exercise for one minute

_____
_____
_____
_____Eve

ning: Cleaning and storing

Light exercise like yoga or a brisk walk

10 reasons for feeling grateful

Write the date before each day

Wake up in gratitude

Day 67: _____

Exercise " I love myself " in front of the mirror in the morning for at least 2 minutes

Silence for at least 5 minutes

Visualize for 10-15 minutes

Imagine spending $3000

Repeat your 300 affirmations

Below is to serve as a diary of all signs of abundance you see.

Morning breathing exercise for one minute

_____
_____
_____

Lunch breathing exercise for one minute
Your promise and prayer

_____
_____
_____
_____
_____
_____
_____

Supper breathing exercise for one minute

_____
_____
_____
_____Eve

ning: Cleaning and storing
Light exercise like yoga or a brisk walk
10 reasons for feeling grateful
Write the date before each day

Wake up in gratitude

Day 68: _____

Exercise " I love myself " in front of the mirror in the morning for at least 2 minutes

Silence for at least 5 minutes

Visualize for 10-15 minutes

Imagine spending $3000

Repeat your 300 affirmations

Below is to serve as a diary of all signs of abundance you see.

Morning breathing exercise for one minute

_____

_____

_____

Lunch breathing exercise for one minute

Your promise and prayer

_____

_____

_____

_____

_____

_____

_____

Supper breathing exercise for one minute

_____

_____

_____

_____Eve

ning: Cleaning and storing

Light exercise like yoga or a brisk walk

10 reasons for feeling grateful

Write the date before each day

Wake up in gratitude

Day 69: _____

Exercise " I love myself " in front of the mirror in the morning for at least 2 minutes

Silence for at least 5 minutes

Visualize for 10-15 minutes

Imagine spending $3000

Repeat your 300 affirmations

Below is to serve as a diary of all signs of abundance you see.

Morning breathing exercise for one minute

_____
_____
_____

Lunch breathing exercise for one minute
Your promise and prayer

_____
_____
_____
_____
_____
_____
_____

Supper breathing exercise for one minute

_____
_____
_____
_____Eve

ning: Cleaning and storing

Light exercise like yoga or a brisk walk

10 reasons for feeling grateful

Brainstorm on how to acquire more money:

_____

_____

_____

_____

_____

_____

_____

_____

_____

_____

_____

_____

_____

_____

_____

_____

_____

_____

_____

_____

_____

_____

_____

_____

_____

_____

_____

_____

_____

_____

Great! 2/3 of your program is done. How do you feel?

Do you feel emotionally lighter? Do you read

regularly why you want to be rich? Do you notice more evidence of wealth in your life? Have you already started to develop an idea that could earn you money?

Have you recently received compliments? Do you feel better inside? I'm sure you look great! I'm sure you reflect the light of success!

Raise your head and walk straight! You have to be proud of who you are! YOU ARE AWESOME I LOVE YOU !!!

Enter below the times when you didn't complete the exercises and promise to do better:

_____

_____

_____

_____

_____

_____

_____

_____

_____

In week 10, you will better manage your time to work on your priorities. Every day, you'll make a list of everything you need to do to increase your finances.

It may be that you have to pay your bills, find a job that pays more, take courses to increase your knowledge in order to be paid more ...

This list will give rise to a list of all you need to do

in the day to improve your financial situation.

Do not worry about the length of the list. I want you to take three of these elements, the ones you really intend to do and write them in this book.

I want this to become a daily habit. It will only take 5 minutes at most. In deciding to do, you become aware and can speed up the co-creative process with the Universe.

We can do it !! Are you ready?

Say YES
Say YES
Say YES !!!!!

I can do it
I can do it
I WILL DO IT !!!

Write the date before each day

Wake up in gratitude

Day 70: _____

Exercise " I love myself " in front of the mirror in the morning for at least 2 minutes
Meditation for at least 10 minutes
Visualize for 10-15 minutes
Imagine spending $3000
Repeat your 300 affirmations

Below is to serve as a diary of all signs of abundance you see.

Morning breathing exercise for one minute

_____
_____
_____

Lunch breathing exercise for one minute
Your promise and prayer

_____
_____
_____
_____
_____

Supper breathing exercise for one minute

_____
_____
_____
_____Eve

ning: Cleaning and storing
Light exercise like yoga or a brisk walk
10 reasons for feeling grateful
3 things you will do tomorrow to improve your finances
Write the date before each day

Wake up in gratitude

Day 71: _____

Exercise " I love myself " in front of the mirror in the morning for at least 2 minutes
Meditation for at least 10 minutes
Visualize for 10-15 minutes
Imagine spending $3000
Repeat your 300 affirmations

Below is to serve as a diary of all signs of abundance you see.

Morning breathing exercise for one minute

_____
_____
_____

Lunch breathing exercise for one minute
Your promise and prayer

_____
_____
_____
_____
_____

Supper breathing exercise for one minute

_____
_____
_____
_____Eve
ning: Cleaning and storing
Light exercise like yoga or a brisk walk
10 reasons for feeling grateful
3 things you will do tomorrow to improve your finances
Write the date before each day

Wake up in gratitude

Day 72: _____

Exercise " I love myself " in front of the mirror in the morning for at least 2 minutes
Meditation for at least 10 minutes
Visualize for 10-15 minutes
Imagine spending $3000
Repeat your 300 affirmations

Below is to serve as a diary of all signs of abundance you see.

Morning breathing exercise for one minute

_____
_____
_____

Lunch breathing exercise for one minute
Your promise and prayer

_____
_____
_____
_____
_____

Supper breathing exercise for one minute

_____
_____
_____
_____Eve
ning: Cleaning and storing
Light exercise like yoga or a brisk walk
10 reasons for feeling grateful
3 things you will do tomorrow to improve your finances
Write the date before each day

Wake up in gratitude

Day 73: _____

Exercise " I love myself " in front of the mirror in the morning for at least 2 minutes
Meditation for at least 10 minutes
Visualize for 10-15 minutes
Imagine spending $3000
Repeat your 300 affirmations

Below is to serve as a diary of all signs of abundance you see.

Morning breathing exercise for one minute

_____
_____
_____

Lunch breathing exercise for one minute
Your promise and prayer

_____
_____
_____
_____
_____

Supper breathing exercise for one minute

_____
_____
_____
                                                    Eve
ning: Cleaning and storing
Light exercise like yoga or a brisk walk
10 reasons for feeling grateful
3 things you will do tomorrow to improve your finances
Write the date before each day

Wake up in gratitude

Day 74: _____

Exercise " I love myself " in front of the mirror in the morning for at least 2 minutes
Meditation for at least 10 minutes
Visualize for 10-15 minutes
Imagine spending $3000
Repeat your 300 affirmations

Below is to serve as a diary of all signs of abundance you see.

Morning breathing exercise for one minute

_____
_____
_____

Lunch breathing exercise for one minute
Your promise and prayer

_____
_____
_____
_____
_____

Supper breathing exercise for one minute

_____
_____
_____
_____Eve
ning: Cleaning and storing
Light exercise like yoga or a brisk walk
10 reasons for feeling grateful
3 things you will do tomorrow to improve your finances
Write the date before each day

Wake up in gratitude

Day 75: _____

Exercise " I love myself " in front of the mirror in the morning for at least 2 minutes
Meditation for at least 10 minutes
Visualize for 10-15 minutes
Imagine spending $3000
Repeat your 300 affirmations

Below is to serve as a diary of all signs of abundance you see.

Morning breathing exercise for one minute

_____
_____
_____

Lunch breathing exercise for one minute
Your promise and prayer

_____
_____
_____
_____
_____

Supper breathing exercise for one minute

_____
_____
_____
_____Eve
ning: Cleaning and storing
Light exercise like yoga or a brisk walk
10 reasons for feeling grateful
3 things you will do tomorrow to improve your finances
Write the date before each day

Wake up in gratitude

Day 76: _____

Exercise " I love myself " in front of the mirror in the morning for at least 2 minutes
Meditation for at least 10 minutes
Visualize for 10-15 minutes
Imagine spending $3000
Repeat your 300 affirmations

Below is to serve as a diary of all signs of abundance you see.

Morning breathing exercise for one minute

_____
_____
_____

Lunch breathing exercise for one minute
Your promise and prayer

_____
_____
_____
_____
_____

Supper breathing exercise for one minute

_____
_____
_____
Evening: Cleaning and storing
Light exercise like yoga or a brisk walk
10 reasons for feeling grateful
3 things you will do tomorrow to improve your finances
Brainstorm all ideas that can lead you towards more abundance

_____
_____
_____

_____
_____
_____
_____
_____
_____
_____
_____
_____
_____
_____
_____
_____
_____
_____
_____
_____
_____
_____
_____
_____
_____
_____
_____
_____
_____
_____
_____
_____

How do you feel? If you follow my advice, you must surely feel much better! You are amazing!

Even if you are only doing half of what I asked you, that's already much more than what you did in the past.

Think about the reasons that prevent you from doing your best. Create a plan to get rid of the excuses that prevent you from moving forward.

You deserve the best in life. Never forget that!

Enter below the times when you almost and you promise to do better:

_____
_____
_____
_____
_____
_____
_____

Week eleven. This week focuses on the theme of forgiveness. I ask you to do just that, forgive. Every day, let go of a little hate, a little resentment, some anger ...

You will do this in two steps. In the first, you're going to name the person who you believe has done you wrong. You will describe in the most amount of words and possible feelings which made you suffer in the behavior of this person.

You will let go of hatred, anger, sadness ... It is not necessary to accept what the other did. You want to get rid of your rage and resentment. Not because you want to see that person again. Forgive to free yourself from the past. The fact that you are angry makes no difference in the life of that person. This anger affects you. Freeing you from this pain, you lighten your heart.

In part two, I want you to do the same for you. Write yourself a love letter forgiving your past mistakes. Forgive yourself for allowing in your life these negative people who made you suffer. Forgive yourself for having lived in suffering and your past mistakes. Let go of everything!

God loves you and I love you too. You can do this! Stop every night and write, at least partially, what you want to forgive. Every day, release a little more of the past pain.

We can do it !! Are you ready?

Say YES
Say YES
Say YES !!!!!

I can do it
I can do it
I WILL DO IT !!!

Write the date before each day

Wake up in gratitude

Day 77: _____
Exercise " I love myself " in front of the mirror in the morning for at least 2 minutes
Meditation for at least 10 minutes
Visualize for 10-15 minutes

Imagine spending $3000
Repeat your 300 affirmations

Below is to serve as a diary of all signs of abundance
you see.

Morning breathing exercise for one minute

_____

_____

_____

Lunch breathing exercise for one minute
Your promise and prayer

_____

_____

_____

_____

Supper breathing exercise for one minute

_____

_____

_____E

vening: Cleaning and storing
Light exercise like yoga or a brisk walk
10 reasons for feeling grateful
3 things you will do tomorrow to improve your
finances
A moment of forgiveness

Write the date before each day

Wake up in gratitude

Day 78: _____
Exercise " I love myself " in front of the mirror in the
morning for at least 2 minutes
Meditation for at least 10 minutes
Visualize for 10-15 minutes

Imagine spending $3000
Repeat your 300 affirmations

Below is to serve as a diary of all signs of abundance you see.

Morning breathing exercise for one minute

_____
_____
_____

Lunch breathing exercise for one minute
Your promise and prayer

_____
_____
_____
_____

Supper breathing exercise for one minute

_____
_____
_____E

vening: Cleaning and storing
Light exercise like yoga or a brisk walk
10 reasons for feeling grateful
3 things you will do tomorrow to improve your finances
A moment of forgiveness

Write the date before each day

Wake up in gratitude

Day 79: _____
Exercise " I love myself " in front of the mirror in the morning for at least 2 minutes
Meditation for at least 10 minutes
Visualize for 10-15 minutes

Imagine spending $3000
Repeat your 300 affirmations

Below is to serve as a diary of all signs of abundance you see.

Morning breathing exercise for one minute

_____
_____
_____

Lunch breathing exercise for one minute
Your promise and prayer

_____
_____
_____
_____

Supper breathing exercise for one minute

_____
_____
_____E

vening: Cleaning and storing
Light exercise like yoga or a brisk walk
10 reasons for feeling grateful
3 things you will do tomorrow to improve your finances
A moment of forgiveness

Write the date before each day

Wake up in gratitude

Day 80: _____

Exercise " I love myself " in front of the mirror in the morning for at least 2 minutes
Meditation for at least 10 minutes
Visualize for 10-15 minutes

Imagine spending $3000
Repeat your 300 affirmations

Below is to serve as a diary of all signs of abundance you see.

Morning breathing exercise for one minute

_____
_____
_____

Lunch breathing exercise for one minute
Your promise and prayer

_____
_____
_____
_____

Supper breathing exercise for one minute

_____
_____
_____ E

vening: Cleaning and storing
Light exercise like yoga or a brisk walk
10 reasons for feeling grateful
3 things you will do tomorrow to improve your finances
A moment of forgiveness

Write the date before each day

Wake up in gratitude

Day 81: _____
Exercise " I love myself " in front of the mirror in the morning for at least 2 minutes
Meditation for at least 10 minutes
Visualize for 10-15 minutes

Imagine spending $3000
Repeat your 300 affirmations

Below is to serve as a diary of all signs of abundance you see.

Morning breathing exercise for one minute

_____
_____
_____

Lunch breathing exercise for one minute
Your promise and prayer

_____
_____
_____
_____

Supper breathing exercise for one minute

_____
_____
_____E

vening: Cleaning and storing
Light exercise like yoga or a brisk walk
10 reasons for feeling grateful
3 things you will do tomorrow to improve your finances
A moment of forgiveness

Write the date before each day

Wake up in gratitude

Day 82: _____
Exercise " I love myself " in front of the mirror in the morning for at least 2 minutes
Meditation for at least 10 minutes
Visualize for 10-15 minutes

Imagine spending $3000
Repeat your 300 affirmations

Below is to serve as a diary of all signs of abundance you see.

Morning breathing exercise for one minute

_____
_____
_____

Lunch breathing exercise for one minute
Your promise and prayer

_____
_____
_____
_____

Supper breathing exercise for one minute

_____
_____
_____E

vening: Cleaning and storing
Light exercise like yoga or a brisk walk
10 reasons for feeling grateful
3 things you will do tomorrow to improve your finances
A moment of forgiveness

Write the date before each day

Wake up in gratitude

Day 83: _____
Exercise " I love myself " in front of the mirror in the morning for at least 2 minutes
Meditation for at least 10 minutes
Visualize for 10-15 minutes

Imagine spending $3000
Repeat your 300 affirmations

Below is to serve as a diary of all signs of abundance you see.

Morning breathing exercise for one minute

_____

_____

_____

Lunch breathing exercise for one minute
Your promise and prayer

_____

_____

_____

_____

Supper breathing exercise for one minute

_____

_____

_____E

vening: Cleaning and storing
Light exercise like yoga or a brisk walk
10 reasons for feeling grateful
3 things you will do tomorrow to improve your finances
A moment of forgiveness

Brainstorm of all the things I can do to improve my financial situation

_____

_____

_____

_____

_____

_____

_____

_____
_____
_____
_____
_____
_____
_____
_____
_____
_____
_____
_____
_____
_____
_____
_____
_____
_____
_____
_____
_____
_____
_____

How do you feel? Have you been able to forgive someone in particular partially or completely? Sometimes this can prove to be a long process. Forgive small events to start before you tackle the most important clashes.

You deserve to live in peace and peace can only be found when you have no more attachment to past pain. Do not do it to please others, but because you will free yourself from these feelings of anger and hatred.

I love you and, therefore, I wish your success! I hope you understand. I would not have spent my time creating this if I did not love you.

Write below what you find most difficult to allow yourself to move forward:

_____

_____

_____

_____

_____

_____

_____

_____

You're almost there ... Twelfth week! This week is going to be either very easy or very difficult. In all ways, you have arrived this far, you should be able to take that step !

You can be the superhero and you know it! Others arrived there and so can you!

This week, you will put your hand on your heart and say loud and clear your goal as a solemn promise that you made. If you have not yet reached this goal, you need to let go and have faith in the Universe that you will reach that goal. Do not change your purpose or goal, stay on course. You will get there. Believe me !!!

To learn more about letting go, I suggest you obtain my complete method called "Know it all to have it all" http://attractitude.us.

LET'S DO IT !! Are you ready?

Say YES
Say YES
Say YES !!!!!

I can do it
I can do it
I WILL DO IT !!!

Write the date before each day

Wake up in gratitude

Day 84: _____
Exercise " I love myself " in front of the mirror in the
morning for at least 2 minutes
Solemn promise hand on heart
Meditation for at least 10 minutes
Visualize for 10-15 minutes
Imagine spending $3000
Repeat your 300 affirmations

Below is to serve as a diary of all signs of abundance you see.

Morning breathing exercise for one minute

_____

_____

_____

Lunch breathing exercise for one minute
Your promise and prayer

_____

_____

_____

_Supper breathing exercise for one minute

_____

_____

_____E

vening: Cleaning and storing
Light exercise like yoga or a brisk walk
10 reasons for feeling grateful
3 things you will do tomorrow to improve your finances
A moment of forgiveness

Write the date before each day

Wake up in gratitude

Day 85: _____
Exercise " I love myself " in front of the mirror in the morning for at least 2 minutes
Solemn promise hand on heart
Meditation for at least 10 minutes
Visualize for 10-15 minutes
Imagine spending $3000
Repeat your 300 affirmations

Below is to serve as a diary of all signs of abundance you see.

Morning breathing exercise for one minute

_____
_____
_____

Lunch breathing exercise for one minute
Your promise and prayer

_____
_____
_____

_Supper breathing exercise for one minute

_____
_____
_____E

vening: Cleaning and storing
Light exercise like yoga or a brisk walk
10 reasons for feeling grateful
3 things you will do tomorrow to improve your finances
A moment of forgiveness

Write the date before each day

Wake up in gratitude

Day 86: _____
Exercise " I love myself " in front of the mirror in the morning for at least 2 minutes
Solemn promise hand on heart
Meditation for at least 10 minutes
Visualize for 10-15 minutes
Imagine spending $3000
Repeat your 300 affirmations

Below is to serve as a diary of all signs of abundance you see.

Morning breathing exercise for one minute

_____
_____
_____

Lunch breathing exercise for one minute
Your promise and prayer

_____
_____
_____

_Supper breathing exercise for one minute

_____
_____
_____E

vening: Cleaning and storing
Light exercise like yoga or a brisk walk
10 reasons for feeling grateful
3 things you will do tomorrow to improve your finances
A moment of forgiveness

Write the date before each day

Wake up in gratitude

Day 87: _____
Exercise " I love myself " in front of the mirror in the morning for at least 2 minutes
Solemn promise hand on heart
Meditation for at least 10 minutes
Visualize for 10-15 minutes
Imagine spending $3000
Repeat your 300 affirmations

Below is to serve as a diary of all signs of abundance you see.

Morning breathing exercise for one minute

_____

_____

_____

Lunch breathing exercise for one minute
Your promise and prayer

_____

_____

_____

_Supper breathing exercise for one minute

_____

_____

_____E

vening: Cleaning and storing
Light exercise like yoga or a brisk walk
10 reasons for feeling grateful
3 things you will do tomorrow to improve your finances
A moment of forgiveness

Write the date before each day

Wake up in gratitude

Day 88: _____
Exercise " I love myself " in front of the mirror in the morning for at least 2 minutes
Solemn promise hand on heart
Meditation for at least 10 minutes
Visualize for 10-15 minutes
Imagine spending $3000
Repeat your 300 affirmations

Below is to serve as a diary of all signs of abundance you see.

Morning breathing exercise for one minute

_____
_____
_____

Lunch breathing exercise for one minute
Your promise and prayer

_____
_____
_____

_Supper breathing exercise for one minute

_____
_____
_____E

vening: Cleaning and storing
Light exercise like yoga or a brisk walk
10 reasons for feeling grateful
3 things you will do tomorrow to improve your finances
A moment of forgiveness

Write the date before each day

Wake up in gratitude

Day 89: _____
Exercise " I love myself " in front of the mirror in the morning for at least 2 minutes
Solemn promise hand on heart
Meditation for at least 10 minutes
Visualize for 10-15 minutes
Imagine spending $3000
Repeat your 300 affirmations

Below is to serve as a diary of all signs of abundance you see.

Morning breathing exercise for one minute

_____
_____
_____

Lunch breathing exercise for one minute
Your promise and prayer

_____
_____
_____

_Supper breathing exercise for one minute

_____
_____
_____E

vening: Cleaning and storing
Light exercise like yoga or a brisk walk
10 reasons for feeling grateful
3 things you will do tomorrow to improve your finances
A moment of forgiveness

Write the date before each day

Wake up in gratitude

Day 90: _____
Exercise " I love myself " in front of the mirror in the morning for at least 2 minutes
Solemn promise hand on heart
Meditation for at least 10 minutes
Visualize for 10-15 minutes
Imagine spending $3000
Repeat your 300 affirmations

Below is to serve as a diary of all signs of abundance you see.

Morning breathing exercise for one minute

_____
_____
_____

Lunch breathing exercise for one minute
Your promise and prayer

_____
_____
_____

_Supper breathing exercise for one minute

_____
_____
_____E

vening: Cleaning and storing
Light exercise like yoga or a brisk walk
10 reasons for feeling grateful
3 things you will do tomorrow to improve your finances
A moment of forgiveness

Brainstorm of what can be done to improve my financial life

_____
_____
_____
_____
_____
_____
_____
_____
_____
_____

_____
_____
_____
_____
_____
_____
_____
_____
_____
_____
_____
_____
_____
_____
_____
_____
_____
_____
_____
_____

Day 91: _____

CELEBRATE !! REJOICE !!

The more you put effort into these practices the more your results will be impressive. Continue to pay attention to money and you how you can earn it. Live with relief. Do not let concerns take over your life. Money is only part of a whole and each facet of your life is important. Remember to keep this balance by continuing to practice gratitude on everything you receive.

Repeat the exercises as and when you need it.

Persevere !!!

I LOVE YOU!

CONCLUSION

My dear friends, I hope you enjoyed this journey to your success. Three months have already passed.

WOW!

I hope you have followed all the instructions. I really wish you reach your goals and live happy in abundance and prosperity.

I want you to take the time to go back and observe your progress, notice how you have evolved. You have suffered. You have persevered and now you have won!

Congratulations!

Stay on course !!

If you follow this program, you should be on track or already rich!

Keep me posted on your progress
slavica@attractitude.us
Or our website : http ://attractitudeus/

I love you !!! God bless

ABOUT THE AUTHOR

Slavica Bogdanov is a success life coach and artist that has published over 25 books, including 3 bestsellers, and whose expertise has helped thousands worldwide.

Born in Belgrade, raised in Paris, Slavica comes from a European family of entrepreneurs who believed hard working was the way to success. She moved to Canada where she completed a Master's Degree in History of Communications at the University of Montreal. She worked mostly in medias such as radio and print. She has traveled a lot, mostly to Europe, Americas, and North Africa. A serial entrepreneur, she has proven many times over that any dream is achievable with the proper method and she created her own formula for rapidly accessing any dream and making it real.

Slavica's latest book, *From Bankrupt to Wealthy*, is the most comprehensive book written to date about achieving financial success no matter where you are financially. Slavica focuses on what she calls, "the three pillars:" self-esteem, goal setting, and time management. Her method and life are about "everything is possible." With her mantra for life, she works to inspire, motivate and empower as many as possible to live life to their full potential. She also encompasses the laws of attraction and prosperity, and developed her own method of commanding one's brain to achieve success. She boasts a 90 percent success rate with her life coaching and has a guarantee that that anyone's life can significantly and permanently improve within 30 days if her methods are utilized entirely